Employment transitions of older workers

The role of flexible employment in maintaining labour market participation and promoting job quality

Stephen Lissenburgh and Deborah Smeaton

The POLICY
P P
PRESS

First published in Great Britain in March 2003 by

The Policy Press
Fourth Floor, Beacon House
Queen's Road
Bristol BS8 1QU
UK

Tel no +44 (0)117 331 4054
Fax no +44 (0)117 331 4093
E-mail tpp@bristol.ac.uk
www.policypress.org.uk

Published for the Joseph Rowntree Foundation by The Policy Press

ISBN 1 86134 475 9

Stephen Lissenburgh is Principal Research Fellow and **Deborah Smeaton** is Research Fellow, both at the Policy Studies Institute, London.

The **Joseph Rowntree Foundation** has supported this project as part of its programme of research and innovative development projects, which it hopes will be of value to policy makers, practitioners and service users. The facts presented and views expressed in this report are, however, those of the authors and not necessarily those of the Foundation.

Cover design by Qube Design Associates, Bristol
Printed in Great Britain by Hobbs the Printers Ltd, Southampton

Contents

List of tables and figures

Tables

Figure

Acknowledgements

The study reported here was funded by the
Joseph Rowntree Foundation under its
'Transitions after 50' programme. The authors are
grateful for the Foundation's financial support,
and for the encouragement and practical
assistance provided by Mark Hinman, the project
manager. We are also most grateful for the
valuable advice and ideas that were provided
throughout the duration of the study by the
Advisory Group established by the Foundation
and by Donald Hirsch, the Programme Adviser.

The data used in this publication were drawn
from the Labour Force Survey (LFS) and the
Working in Britain (WiB) survey. Material from
the LFS was made available through the Office
for National Statistics and the Data Archive, and
has been used by permission of the Controller of
Her Majesty's Stationery Office. The WiB survey
was conceived and produced from a
collaborative project between the Policy Studies
Institute and the London School of Economics
and Political Science, funded by the Economic
and Social Research Council as part of its 'Future
of Work' programme. Project team members
include Michael White, Deborah Smeaton,
Stephen Hill, Patrick McGovern and Colin Mills.
The data fieldwork was carried out by System 3.
Neither the original collectors of these data nor
the Data Archive bear any responsibility for the
analyses or interpretations presented here.

As ever, responsibility for the content and
conclusions of the report rests solely with the
authors.

Summary

The labour market experiences of older workers have changed markedly in recent decades. Men in particular are on average leaving work earlier. People who lose their jobs in their fifties and sixties find it increasingly difficult to re-establish themselves in a career. Economic inactivity among this age group has grown, whether resulting from people taking early retirement or from people losing their jobs and being discouraged in the search for a new one.

Many commentators have been asking whether there are alternatives to the experience of an abrupt and perhaps premature departure from work – a form of transition that can prevent valuable economic potential from being tapped in a period in which the younger labour force will be shrinking. One possibility is for more use to be made of flexible forms of work that can bridge the gap between a steady career job and retirement. This report explores the experience so far of such 'bridge' jobs in the wider context of the types of transition that are being made by people leaving work early. Specifically, it uses the Labour Force Survey (LFS) to examine the characteristics and experiences of those leaving permanent jobs between age 50 and state retirement age, looks at factors associated with a move to temporary, part-time or self-employment, and considers the qualities of these alternative forms of work.

The key findings of the research were as follows.

The factors associated with exits from permanent full-time employment

The factors associated with exits from permanent full-time employment among men are redolent of the 'two nations in early retirement' notion familiar in this field of research. On the one hand, certain advantages appear to enable some people to leave work as a positive choice. Workers over 50 are more likely to leave jobs if they have been with their present employer for longer, and are therefore more likely to have accumulated savings and pension entitlements. So are those who have paid off their mortgages. On the other hand, people are more likely to leave full-time jobs if they have health problems, especially low-paid men. For this group, 'early retirement' is more likely to be the result of an inability to stay in employment, rather than a positive choice to leave it. However, the most important factor of all in explaining male exits from permanent full-time employment is age, with the likelihood of exit increasing as the state pension age draws near. While we do not have the data to test whether this is due to age discrimination, it is certainly consistent with that interpretation.

Advancing age is also the factor associated most strongly with an increased likelihood of exit from permanent full-time employment among older women. As with men, health problems and the outright ownership of property are also important. Unlike men, however, older women are also more likely to stay in permanent full-time employment if they are in relatively good jobs. Women who are managers, supervisors or have recently received job-related training, are less likely to leave their jobs. While this may be evidence of a more positive labour market environment for older women, whose employment rates have actually increased since 1997, it may also reflect the weaker influence for women of the wealth-related factors that play a role in encouraging men to leave work. Time with their current employer had no effect on women's exit probability, for example, which may reflect women's less substantial occupational pension entitlements.

The factors associated with movement into flexible employment

Many of the factors most strongly associated with leaving a permanent full-time job also make it more likely that people leave work altogether rather than obtain flexible employment. Of consistent importance here are time spent with the current employer, age, health problems and outright ownership of property. However, there are a number of positive factors that encourage older workers to move into flexible employment rather than leaving the workforce, but these vary according to gender and to the type of flexible employment under consideration. For example, men with intermediate-level qualifications and higher pay are more likely to move into self-employment, whereas women with higher degrees are more likely to move into temporary employment. Men with intermediate-level qualifications and recent experience of training are more likely to enter part-time employment, but the same does not apply to women. Reductions in hours while remaining in permanent full-time employment are more common for managers and professionals and among those with qualifications. This is true for both men and women.

The quality of flexible employment

Measured against the yardstick of permanent full-time employment, the quality of flexible employment varies according to the type of flexible employment under consideration. There is also a substantial amount of variation in quality *within* particular categories of flexible employment.

Self-employment offers job quality most comparable to that enjoyed by permanent full-time employees. It is shown to be relatively stable, and the self-employed reported high levels of job satisfaction and, as one would expect, had high levels of control over how they spent their time. However, only the more advantaged self-employed workers – those who were professionals or owners of limited businesses – had earnings profiles that were superior to those of permanent full-time employees.

Temporary employment is rated next in terms of job quality. As one might expect, it is less stable than permanent full-time employment, but temporary workers were more likely to receive training. However, earning potential in temporary employment varies substantially according to the type of work under consideration. Whereas those on fixed-term contracts earned more than comparable permanent full-time employees, this was not the case for casual or agency temps. These workers on fixed-term contracts were more likely to be managers or professionals.

Part-time employment offers the poorest job quality among the three types of flexible employment, especially regarding stability and training opportunities, where it is inferior to permanent full-time employment for both men and women.

Policy questions

The research is able to provide some answers to three broad policy questions.

What can be done to promote the maintenance of older workers in permanent full-time employment?

Workers aged between 50 and state pension age are most likely to leave permanent full-time employment if they are older or have health problems. These factors are particularly important for men. There are a number of existing policy initiatives that can potentially promote the maintenance of older workers in permanent full-time employment where they have these characteristics, but in other respects there are policy gaps that need to be filled.

While the New Deal for Disabled People seeks to encourage sick or disabled people to re-enter work when they are out of the labour market, of more relevance to this discussion are policies that help people with health problems to *remain* in work. Examples of such policies are the Job Retention and Rehabilitation Pilots, developed by the Department for Education and Skills. These initiatives target people who are in work but have a health problem and seek to prevent people from losing their jobs either by organising early medical intervention or by reorganising employment to minimise the consequences of the health problem for work performance. While such initiatives are at an early stage of development, our findings on the negative effects of health problems on likelihood of staying in permanent full-time employment suggest they have a potentially important role.

The fact that the chances of leaving permanent full-time employment increase with age, even after controlling for a wide range of other factors, does not provide direct evidence of age discrimination but is certainly consistent with it. The government is currently seeking to tackle age discrimination through the non-statutory Code of Practice on Age Diversity in Employment, but with the adoption by the European Council of Ministers of the Employment Directive on Equal Treatment, this is due to be fortified by a legislative approach. Specifically, the government is due to introduce antidiscrimination legislation relating to age by 2006. While attempts to outlaw age discrimination have met with difficulties, there is at least the potential that such policies would reduce the number of older workers making exits from permanent full-time employment.

The study found that older women were less likely to leave permanent full-time employment if they were in relatively good jobs. As such, the adoption or improvement of equal opportunities policies, designed to advance women's relative position in the workplace, would be likely to increase employment retention.

What can be done to encourage older workers to move into flexible employment?

While this is not universally the case, there was a strong tendency in this study for older workers with relatively high levels of human capital and who had enjoyed a relatively good permanent full-time job to move into flexible employment rather than leaving work when moving out of permanent full-time employment. Therefore, policies designed to improve the human capital of older workers and to help them maintain their position in the occupational hierarchy would be likely to encourage them to enter flexible employment as a bridge to retirement, rather than moving out of the workforce.

Among current government policies, New Deal 50 Plus offers an Employment Credit to boost pay and an in-work training grant to help boost human capital, but this programme is only available to older people who have been out of work and claiming benefits for at least six months. This research suggests that similar initiatives might be effective if made available to older people who are still in work. While older workers will of course benefit from the Working Tax Credit, which will boost take-home pay for those on lower wages, there is an argument that this should be available on a more generous basis to older workers. This is because they have a relatively high probability of exiting work compared to younger workers, with all that follows in terms of lost tax revenues and, in many cases, additional benefit payments. If a more generous Working Tax Credit for older workers could reduce the employment rate differential between older and younger workers, it would be at least partly self-financing. Policies to encourage employment retention and advancement for people already in work have become an important feature of employment policy in many US states, and, according to the findings of this research, older workers in the UK would be likely to benefit from similar initiatives. The importance of training in encouraging older workers to enter some categories of flexible employment also suggests that the lifelong learning and active ageing agendas continue to be relevant and likely to yield positive results if pursued effectively.

What can be done to improve the quality of flexible employment?

The greatest shortfalls in job quality were to be found among casual and agency temporary work and in part-time work as a whole. Policies to improve the quality of flexible employment for older workers would be most effective, therefore, if focused specifically on these categories. Given the delay in the EU Directive on Temporary Agency Work, it has been argued by organisations such as the Trades' Union Congress that the UK government should take a more proactive approach and extend the employment protection proposed for those on fixed-term contracts, through the Fixed Term Employees (Prevention of Less Favourable Treatment) Regulations, to all categories of temporary worker. In doing this, the government would clearly need to have regard to the possible negative impact such regulation might have upon employers' willingness to provide temporary jobs and further research is therefore required on this. An alternative approach likely to yield some degree of success would be to boost the human capital and earning capacity of older workers more generally, as suggested above, because this in itself would be likely to have some positive impact on the quality of flexible employment. It may be that policies such as increasing the National Minimum Wage would be of more benefit for older workers in part-time jobs, since they would benefit disproportionately from such action.

Employment transitions of older workers: introduction

The labour market experiences of older workers have changed markedly in recent decades. Men in particular are on average leaving work earlier. People who lose their jobs in their fifties and sixties have found it increasingly difficult to re-establish themselves in a career. Economic inactivity among this age group has grown, whether resulting from people taking early retirement or from people losing their jobs and being discouraged in the search for a new one.

Many commentators have been asking whether there are alternatives to the experience of an abrupt and perhaps premature departure from work – a form of transition that can leave individuals feeling disoriented and disappointed, and which can prevent their valuable economic potential from being tapped in a period in which the younger labour force will be shrinking. One possibility is for more use to be made of flexible forms of work that can bridge the gap between a steady career job and retirement. This report explores the experience so far of such 'bridge' jobs in the wider context of the types of transition that are being made by people leaving work early. Specifically, it examines characteristics and experiences of those leaving permanent jobs between age 50 and retirement age, looks at factors associated with a move to temporary, part-time or self-employment and considers the qualities of these alternative forms of work.

The context: falling employment rates

Between 1979 and 1997, the employment prospects of older people (aged 50 and above) underwent a number of changes. Most notably, the employment rate for men dropped by 16 percentage points, while, among women, it rose five percentage points, compared to a ten percentage point rise in the employment rate for women aged 18-49 (Labour Force Survey [LFS]). While the decline in employment rates for older men has levelled out over the last five years and the gap in employment rates between younger women and those aged 50 and above has narrowed somewhat (Bardasi and Jenkins, 2002), it remains the case that around a half of all men and a third of women retire before state pension age (Disney et al, 1997). Years in paid employment are being squeezed at both ends of the lifecourse – entry to the labour market occurs later in life with compulsory schooling and further education delaying entry, and enforced or voluntary retirement occurs at younger ages. This reorganisation of patterns of work and non-work is taking place at a time when life expectancy is increasing.

The decline in the employment rate for men aged 50 and above, and the relatively slow increase for older women, has been matched by an increase in the rate of economic inactivity for older men and a decline in the rate of economic inactivity for older women that is slower than that experienced by women aged 18-49. The economic inactivity rate for older men increased by 15 percentage points between 1979 and 1997, while the economic inactivity rate for older women fell by four percentage points, compared with an 11 percentage point fall for women aged 18-49 (LFS). While this increase in the economic inactivity rate for older men and the relatively slow decrease for older women have both been less prevalent in the last five years, this remains a major change in the pattern of labour market participation of people aged 50 and above.

Declining employment rates and increased rates of economic inactivity, especially among older men, have been well documented (McKay and Middleton, 1998; Disney, 1999). Attention has also become focused in recent years on changes in the pattern of employment among older people who *remain* in work. Workers aged 50 and above are less likely to be full-time employees than are younger workers and are more likely to be self-employed or to work as part-time employees (LFS). Older men are also more likely to be in temporary jobs than are younger men. Self-employment, part-time and temporary jobs, when taken after departure from a full-time career position and prior to permanent retirement, are sometimes referred to as 'bridge' jobs, as they have the potential to bridge the gap and prevent premature labour market exit (PIU, 2000). It remains unclear, however, whether these types of 'flexible' employment are able to perform the 'bridging' function described and also whether they provide employment of sufficient quality to be acceptable as an alternative to permanent full-time employment.

Factors encouraging movement out of employment[1]

Why do people move out of work before retirement age? The factors associated with this process are both complex and heterogeneous.

Several studies have found that *health problems* are an important cause of the decline in employment rates among older workers. The survey of retired men conducted by Parker (1980) and Walker's (1985) study of early retirement in Sheffield both found that ill-health had an important influence on the retirement decision. More recently, analyses of the Office for National Statistics Retirement Survey, first conducted in 1988-89 (Meghir and Whitehouse, 1995), suggested that ill-health was one of the main reasons for retirement before state pension age. This finding was confirmed by Tanner's (1997) analysis of the 1994 Retirement Survey, which involved re-interviewing as many respondents as possible from the first wave. She found that over a quarter (27%) of respondents who left the labour force before state pension age cited their own ill-health as the main reason for doing so, with a further 5% attributing the decision to the ill-health of others.[2] This evidence of health problems as an important cause of declining employment rates among older workers has coincided with a substantial increase in the number of people claiming Incapacity Benefit (Taylor et al, 2000). However, Blundell et al (2001), in further analysis of the 1988-89 Retirement Survey, found no relationship between Invalidity Benefit[3] entitlement and early exit.

Some studies have found that the tendency for older workers, especially men, to leave employment before state pension age, varies according to their levels of *qualifications and earnings*. Campbell's (1999) analysis of the first six waves (1991-96) of the British Household Panel Survey (BHPS), for example, found that, although qualifications had no direct effect, older workers in the bottom quarter of the wage distribution had a greater chance of leaving employment than higher paid workers. As lower paid workers are also likely to be relatively unskilled, this is consistent with the shift in labour demand away from older, less skilled workers, which is part of the more general labour demand changes against the less skilled that have occurred over the last 20 years. This shift has been interpreted as due to skill-biased technological change (Machin, 1996). Campbell (1999) found that older workers in the top half of the wage distribution were less likely to leave employment than lower paid workers as long as they did not have occupational pensions. This interaction between earnings and pension entitlement has been found by other researchers, with Meghir and Whitehouse's (1995) analysis of the Retirement Survey finding that higher pay tended to discourage early retirement as long as the individual was not entitled to an occupational or personal pension. The implication of these findings is that higher pay

---

[1] While not exclusively the case, most of the studies described in this section are empirical analyses of UK survey data.

[2] Against this, Casey (1998) cautions that the interpretation of survey findings is made difficult by the fact that some respondents giving retrospective answers may offer 'health' as a more socially acceptable response than some of the other alternatives.

[3] Invalidity Benefit is the predecessor of Incapacity Benefit.

tends to encourage labour market attachment, but that pension entitlement weakens it.

The *industry and occupation in which they are employed* has also been found to impact on whether older workers make exits from the labour force before state pension age. Taylor and Urwin's (1999) analysis of LFS data from 1992, 1993, 1994 and 1996, for example, shows that older men who previously worked in manufacturing or construction were more likely to be unemployed than men from other industrial backgrounds. They also found that older men who previously worked in primary or extraction industries were more likely to be economically inactive due to long-term sickness or disability. Similarly, Campbell's (1999) analyses of the BHPS found that older men were more likely to be working in shrinking industries and that displacement from the labour market was more prevalent in these industries. This is further evidence, therefore, of demand shifts against older workers, especially men. Taylor and Urwin (1999) and Tanner (1997) also found that working in a higher level occupation (for example, as a manager or professional) is associated with a reduced likelihood of leaving employment due to ill-health.

A considerable amount of research has been carried out in recent years on the relationship between *partnership status* and economic activity (Dorsett, 2001). This issue has received relatively little attention, however, in the literature on the labour market participation of older workers, at least as far as British empirical studies are concerned. Tanner (1998), in further analysis of the Retirement Survey, found that older women were more likely than older men to say that they left employment before state pension age because they wanted to retire at the same time as their partner. More extensive analyses of this type of relationship would be a useful enhancement of the literature in this area of research.

A controversial issue in the literature on older workers and the labour market concerns the degree to which declining employment rates among people aged 50 and over are due to *age discrimination*. A number of studies carried out in the 1990s found evidence of age discrimination in employment (Taylor and Walker, 1994; Arrowsmith and McGoldrick, 1996; Hayward et al, 1997). Ageism has also been apparent in many of the early retirement programmes developed by employers and state agencies in recent decades (Casey and Wood, 1994; Taylor and Walker, 1995). These attitudes and policies can be seen to have encouraged older workers, both directly and indirectly, to withdraw from the labour market (Walker and Taylor, 1993). Analysis of the Retirement Survey (Meghir and Whitehouse, 1995) and of the BHPS (Campbell, 1999) has also found that increasing age is associated with an increased risk of early retirement or labour market displacement before state pension age. Against this, McKay and Middleton's (1998) analysis of the 1994-95 Family and Working Lives Survey found that only a relatively small proportion (5%) of people aged 45-69 believed that they had been discriminated against in one or more job applications because they were felt to be too old. However, this low figure may be partly due to the fact that people may be unaware that they have been discriminated against on grounds of age, as they may not, for example, have access to information about the age and other characteristics of fellow job applicants (Campbell, 1999).

Factors encouraging movement into flexible employment

While a number of studies have addressed issues concerning the reasons for declining employment rates among older workers, relatively little attention has been focused on why older workers leaving full-time jobs might *remain* in employment, albeit in a 'flexible' form such as self-employment, part-time or temporary work, rather than permanent full-time employment.[4] Campbell's (1999) analyses of the BHPS address the related issue of the factors associated with *moving back* into paid employment following a displacement. He finds that unemployed people and women looking after their family are more likely to do this than people with long-term illness. Campbell (1999) does not distinguish,

---

[4] While 'flexible' is used as a convenient collective label, we do not suppose that the types of employment to which it refers are in practice altogether flexible, or that they all share the same kind of flexibility. When we speak of them and label them as a group, this is purely for the sake of brevity (White and Forth, 1998).

however, between movements back into flexible rather than permanent full-time employment.

The quality of flexible employment

Since flexible employment is being considered as a potential means of helping older workers to remain in the labour market, providing a bridge between permanent full-time work and retirement, it is important to assess the quality of flexible employment compared with permanent full-time work. Several researchers have found an association between 'flexible' employment (taken here to include self-employment, part-time employment and temporary employment) and reduced career opportunities, lower levels of job security and lower pay (Reskin and Roos, 1990; Dex et al, 1994; O'Reilly, 1994; Lissenburgh, 1996; Dex and McCulloch, 1997; Gallie et al, 1998). Taylor and Urwin's (2001) analysis of LFS data from Spring 1997 shows that men in temporary jobs were less likely to receive training compared with men in full-time employment, and that women were less likely to receive training in both temporary and part-time jobs, compared with women in full-time employment. This training shortfall in flexible employment may be particularly marked for older workers, since Taylor and Urwin (2001) also found that older workers were much less likely to participate in employer provided training than younger workers. One of the main reasons for this was employer decision making, rather than an individual preference not to undertake training.

The relatively poor quality of flexible jobs is underpinned by the dual labour market perspective, which dates back to the early 1970s with the model of structural segmentation into primary and secondary sectors proposed by Doeringer and Piore (1971). The demand for more flexible labour markets, which gained momentum during the 1980s in response to heightened global competition, gave rise to a renewed interest in the association between job quality and non-standard or flexible employment (Casey, 1991; Beck, 1992; Hutton, 1995; Tilly, 1996; Kalleberg et al, 2000). It has been widely recognised that 'contingent' or non-standard employment contracts are a source of socioeconomic inequality.

These characteristics of flexible employment may fuel the concern that it risks promoting an age-segmented labour force (Taylor and Walker, 1994; OECD, 1995), with older workers shifted into peripheral sectors characterised by lower status and poorer terms and conditions. However, an alternative perspective holds that secondary labour market positions embody employment conditions suitable and appropriate for those with particular labour market orientations.

The focus and method of the research

The research outlined in the remainder of this report has three main elements:

- It analyses the factors associated with exits from permanent full-time employment among a sample of men and women aged between 50 and state pension age.
- It identifies the factors associated with movements from permanent full-time employment to flexible employment for the same sample of older workers.
- It assesses the relative quality of flexible employment, in order to inform thinking concerning whether flexible employment represents a credible alternative to permanent full-time employment for those older workers who might otherwise leave employment before state pension age.

To carry out the research, we have made use of the LFS, exploiting the longitudinal element of the dataset introduced in 1992, by conducting the survey quarterly and tracking individuals over five successive quarters. This survey is a rich dataset using a nationally representative sample of approximately 60,000 households (150,000 individuals) with a response rate of 80-85%. Demographic, educational and economic activity data are collected in considerable detail from individuals aged 16 and above. Each quarter, a new 'wave' of 12,000 households is introduced and the oldest wave leaves, so that 60,000 are interviewed at any one time with each wave or panel being tracked over about 12 months.[5] The ability to monitor changes for individuals over

---

[5] The fifth quarterly interview takes place about 12 months after the first.

time is obviously important for a study of employment transitions.[6]

This study uses a sample of entrants from spring 1997 to summer 2000, to give a sample of just under 43,000 people aged 50 years or more. Using very recently collected survey data enables us to consider whether some of the findings from empirical research in the 1980s and early-to-mid-1990s have continued to be important since that time. It is of particular interest to investigate whether the period since 1997, when the declining employment rates of older workers have tended to level off, has been characterised by any change in the range of factors having an important influence on employment transitions and job quality.

The LFS is underused as a panel dataset and provides distinct advantages in terms of sample size. It also contains a rich variety of information on the socioeconomic characteristics of respondents, which makes it possible for us to investigate many of the issues raised by previous research on older workers and the labour market. The range of information available includes the following:

- information on partner and dependants
- housing tenure
- occupation, industry and sector
- region
- age
- gender
- health
- qualifications
- earnings and hours of work
- time with current employer
- size of workplace

- job characteristics, such as whether the respondent is a manager or supervisor
- the receipt of job-related training.[7]

One important area of information that is not available in the LFS relates to occupational and personal pensions. Previous research has suggested that membership of such pension schemes can encourage older workers to take early retirement (see Disney et al, 1994; Disney, 1996; Blundell et al, 2000; Blundell and Johnson, 1998, 1999; and other studies referred to above) but the LFS does not contain any information that could be used to test whether this continues to be the case in the late 1990s and early 2000s. We attempt to overcome this problem by considering the degree to which years spent with the current employer might be a proxy for occupational pension entitlement, since length of employment, especially in permanent full-time employment, is likely to be positively related to the chances of being in an employer pension scheme.

Another area of research on which we are able to shed little light is the role of age discrimination in explaining why older workers leave permanent full-time employment. Many qualitative and quantitative studies that have asked directly about discrimination have been able to produce findings on this issue, but the LFS does not contain the type of information required to investigate this issue in a satisfactory manner.

The remainder of the report is set out as follows. **Chapter 2** identifies the factors associated with exits from permanent full-time employment among the LFS sample of men and women aged between 50 and state pension age. **Chapter 3** examines the factors associated with movements

---

[6] We necessarily stipulate that, in order to be included in the analyses, an individual must have been a respondent at the first and fifth interviews, at least. As one might expect, this results in a degree of sample attrition. Longitudinal weights to correct for any resultant bias are provided by the Office for National Statistics, which administers the survey. However, we have not used these weights in our analysis as they correct for attrition among the LFS population and not specifically for attrition among the sub-sample of older workers, which has its own particular characteristics. This is consistent with the approach taken by White and Forth (1998) in their analysis of the BHPS.

[7] Where the LFS did not include appropriate data, it was possible to compensate for this to some degree by carrying out supplementary analyses using the Working in Britain (WiB) survey. WiB is a nationally representative survey of 2,500 workers aged 20-60 carried out in 2000. The survey was designed by a team of researchers from the Policy Studies Institute and the London School of Economics and Political Science; it was funded by the Economic and Social Research Council under the phase I 'Future of Work' programme.

from permanent full-time employment to flexible employment for the same sample of older workers. **Chapter 4** assesses the quality of self-employment, temporary employment and part-time employment, relative to permanent full-time employment, in order to consider whether flexible employment represents a credible alternative to permanent full-time employment for those older workers who might otherwise leave the labour force before state pension age. **Chapter 5** outlines the conclusions of the study and considers its policy implications.

Movements out of permanent full-time employment

Introduction

Chapter 1 reviewed evidence, from previous UK empirical studies, of the causes of the overall decline in employment for workers aged between age 50 and retirement age. In this chapter, we use our own research to look more specifically at people who are leaving work in this age range. The chapter is based on an analysis of the factors associated with movement out of *permanent full-time employment* by older workers. This focus on movement out of steady full-time jobs, rather than necessarily out of work altogether, sets the scene for the following chapter, which looks at the subset of these leavers who find alternative, 'flexible' jobs.

Among the LFS cohort used for this study, 11,394 men and 5,141 women were in permanent full-time employment at the first interview (Table 2.1).[1] By the fifth interview, held about a year

after the first, 12% of men and 14% of women were no longer in permanent full-time jobs. More than half (56%) of those respondents who had moved out of permanent full-time jobs had left to unemployment or economic inactivity. In other words, they had made a non-work exit. In examining the factors associated with transitions out of permanent full-time employment, therefore, we are considering in a majority of cases the reasons for moving from work to non-work.[2]

Econometric models were run to identify the factors associated with movements out of permanent full-time employment.[3] These models show the extent to which moving out of permanent full-time employment is associated with particular factors about which data is collected in the survey. Each of these factors is measured at the first interview, so that its value could not have been caused *by* a shift out of permanent full-time employment, rather than vice versa. The explanatory variables included in the model consisted of measures of personal and background characteristics such as age, marital status and partner's economic activity, health problems, highest qualification, the number of dependant children in the household, ethnicity, household tenure and region. This was supplemented by information about the job in

Table 2.1: Movements out of permanent full-time employment, by gender (%)

	Male	Female	All
Not in permanent full-time employment at fifth interview	12	14	12
Still in permanent full-time employment at fifth interview	88	86	88
Base	*11,394*	*5,141*	*16,535*

---

[1] For the purposes of this analysis, respondents are classified as being in permanent full-time employment at the first interview if they are in a permanent full-time job at this time. This definition excludes any respondents who were self-employed in the first quarter. Jobs are defined as permanent according to the perceptions of the respondent.

[2] In Chapter 3, as suggested above, we examine in detail the factors associated with *types* of transition out of permanent full-time employment and make a distinction between work and non-work exits.

[3] Specifically, binary logistic regression models were computed. The dependent variable in each model took the value 1 if a respondent moved out of permanent full-time employment and 0 if they remained in permanent full-time employment.

which respondents were observed during the first interview. This incorporated data on the size of workplace, occupation, industry, sector, the number of years the respondent had been with the current employer and whether they had received any training in the four weeks prior to the first interview. Models were run separately for men and women, so that any gender differences in the factors that were important in explaining exits would be clearly revealed.

Male exits from permanent full-time employment

Table 2.2 shows the factors that are most strongly associated with exits from permanent full-time employment in the male models. The factors are listed according to the importance of the variable, with the most important variable appearing at the top of the table and importance declining as one moves down the table.[4] Thus, the first column of Table 2.2 shows the factors that were found to be most important in explaining movements out of permanent full-time employment. The second column shows the independent impact in terms of percentage points of a one-unit change in each factor on the likelihood of leaving permanent full-time employment in the period under consideration. The third column shows the level of statistical significance of each effect.[5] For the most part, the factors shown by this analysis to be important determinants of movement out of permanent full-time employment by older men are consistent with the findings of previous empirical research on the reasons for declining employment rates among older workers.

The most important factor associated with movement out of permanent full-time employment is age. For each year older that a man was at the first interview, his chances of

---

[4] Full statistical results from these analyses and others are not shown, as these are lengthy. Details can be obtained from the authors on request.

[5] This shows a level of probability at which the effect might have arisen by chance. Thus, a particularly strong or well-specified effect will have a level of significance of 1%, indicating that there is at most a 1% likelihood that it has arisen by chance, whereas somewhat weaker effects would be subject to a 5 or 10% likelihood, and so on.

Table 2.2: Factors encouraging movement out of permanent full-time employment, men

Factor (measured at first interview)	Percentage impact (%)[a]	Level of statistical significance (%)[b]
Age	+17	1
Health problem	+35	1
Owns accommodation outright	+29	1
Partner works	−23	1
Lives in the North[c]	+62	1
Years continuously employed	+12	1
Qualifications (NVQ1-4)	+29-37	5
Worked in electricity, gas and water supply	+58	5
Worked for health authority or NHS Trust hospital	−53	5
Hourly earnings	+13	10

Notes: [a] For example, for each year older that a man was at the first interview, his chances of leaving permanent full-time employment within a year increased by 17%.

[b] For example, there is a 1% or lower probability that the association between age and job exit observed among the sample occurred by chance.

[c] The regional variables used throughout this report are DWP regions, which are as follows: Scotland, Wales, North, North West, Yorkshire and Humberside, West Midlands, Eastern and East Anglia, South West, London and South East.

leaving permanent full-time employment within a year increased by 17%. While the effect of age is partly due to some men reaching state pension age (SPA) by the end of the year, this was the case for less than 3% of the sample. Closer examination of the relationship between age and movement out of permanent full-time employment for men shows a gradual decline in the proportion of men still in permanent full-time employment at the fifth interview, from 93% for those aged 51 at this time to 88% for those aged 59. Then there is a steep decline to 81% for those aged 60, with no further decline until we reach those who passed SPA during the year, of whom only 20% were still in permanent full-time employment at the end of it. This positive relationship between age and employment exit is consistent with similar findings from Meghir and Whitehouse's (1995) analysis of the Retirement Survey and Campbell's (1999) analysis of the BHPS.

The next most important factor after age is the experience of long-term health problems. When men said at the first interview that they had a health problem that had lasted for more than a year, their chances of leaving permanent full-time employment by the end of the year was increased by 35%.[6] Men who were in permanent full-time employment at the first interview but reported health problems were particularly likely to become economically inactive by the time of the fifth interview, with 10% of such men inactive by this time compared with 5% of men who were in permanent full-time employment at the first interview but did not have health problems. The destinations of older workers who left permanent full-time employment are examined in more detail in the next chapter. The role of health problems in exacerbating declining employment rates among older workers, especially men, has of course been emphasised by the existing empirical literature (Tanner, 1997).

Exits from permanent full-time employment are encouraged by an absence of housing costs. When men said at the first interview that they owned their accommodation outright, this increased their chances of exit by 29% compared to those men buying a house with a mortgage. It would appear that freedom from the financial constraints of needing to pay a mortgage weakens the attachment of men to permanent full-time employment after the age of 50, especially when this is combined with the wealth effect of outright home ownership.[7] This is not an issue that has been explored in any depth in previous UK empirical literature.

Male exits from permanent full-time employment are also related to their partnership status and to their partner's activity status at the time of the first interview. Men whose partners were in paid

employment at the time of the first interview, had reduced chances of leaving permanent full-time employment by 23% relative to single men. Men whose partners were economically inactive at the time of the first interview were 18% less likely to exit permanent full-time employment than single men. This evidence is consistent with a considerable body of research that suggests couples' economic activities are interrelated and that partnered men are more likely to remain economically active than single men. Tanner (1998) found a similar result for women, but not for men, in her analysis of the Retirement Survey.

The likelihood of older male workers making exits from permanent full-time employment varies to some degree with the region in which they live, the industrial sector in which they are located and the type of employer for whom they work. Men living in the North at the first interview were 62% more likely to leave permanent full-time employment by the fifth interview than men who lived in London and the South East, even after controlling for other factors associated with this type of exit. Those who lived in Yorkshire and Humberside, the North West and Wales were also more likely to leave permanent full-time employment than men who lived in London and the South East, but the effects for these regions are not so strong. Men working in the energy sector (electricity, gas and water supply) were 58% more likely to leave permanent full-time employment than men who were working in manufacturing at the first interview. In contrast, working for a health authority or NHS Trust hospital reduces a man's chances of leaving permanent full-time employment by 53%.

Higher levels of qualifications and earnings are also associated with an increased likelihood of exit from permanent full-time employment among older male workers. Those whose highest qualification is equivalent to NVQ levels 1-4 were 29-37% more likely to have left permanent full-time employment by the time of the fifth interview, compared with those with no qualifications. Each additional pound earned per hour by men is associated with an increase of 13% in the likelihood of leaving permanent full-time employment by the time of the fifth interview. It is likely that men with higher earnings have more savings than those with less earning power and that these higher savings are

---

[6] Ranking of factors in terms of their importance was determined by the degree to which the factor's effect was statistically significant. Thus, while the percentage impact of having a health problem (at 35%) was larger than that of being one year older (at 17%), the latter effect was more statistically reliable and is thus attributed greater importance.

[7] The absence of dependent children from the household, which would reduce the financial imperative to work and might also therefore have been expected to encourage exits from permanent full-time employment, was taken account of in this analysis but had no effect.

being used to finance early retirement.[8] This finding of a positive relationship between pay and employment exit is not consistent with earlier research (Meghir and Whitehouse, 1995; Campbell, 1999), which found that better paid older workers were somewhat less likely to leave employment than their lower paid counterparts. Importantly, however, these studies controlled for whether the respondent was entitled to an occupational or personal pension and indeed only found that higher pay discouraged employment exit where older workers did *not* have such pension entitlement. As higher paid workers are more likely to have occupational or personal pension entitlement, it is likely that our finding of a positive relationship between pay and employment exit is conflating the effects of pay and pension entitlement.

The final variable that is strongly associated with male exits from permanent full-time employment is the number of years that the respondent has been continuously employed. The chances of leaving permanent full-time employment increase by 12% with each additional year the respondent has been continuously employed. It is worth noting that this effect is measured independently of age, which was of course the most powerful variable in the model. In the absence of a variable identifying whether respondents were part of an occupational pension scheme, years continuously employed is the best proxy we have for this, since permanent full-time workers are often members of occupational pension schemes and their level of entitlements tends to accrue with seniority. The fact that this variable is associated with a greater likelihood of leaving permanent full-time employment is consistent with this interpretation. However, as the previous discussion of earnings and employment exit showed, trying to tease out the effect of pension entitlement in this data is fraught with difficulty in the absence of a definitive measure.

Before moving to a discussion of the female analyses, it is worth noting that the importance of earnings was explored in more detail for men by computing separate models according to their position in the wage distribution, as measured at the first interview. The male wage distribution was divided into three portions for this purpose and models run for the bottom third, middle third and top third of the distribution.[9] This was done to explore whether any of the factors identified as important in the analyses for men as a whole were particularly important, or unimportant, for men with high, medium or low earnings levels.[10]

The effect of health problems in encouraging men to make exits from permanent full-time employment is particularly strong for men in the bottom third of the wage distribution. When these men had health problems, their chances of leaving permanent full-time employment by the fifth interview were increased by 65%, whereas the effect of health problems for medium and higher paid men was only 31-32%. In contrast, the outright ownership of accommodation had a larger effect for medium and especially high earning men compared with those on low earnings. This suggests that there may be a wealth effect associated with this variable, as well as an income effect associated with not having to pay housing costs. More broadly, these findings are redolent of the familiar conception of the 'two nations in early retirement' – with older workers from a disadvantaged background leaving employment involuntarily due to unemployment or ill-health, while their more advantaged counterparts leave voluntarily due to their acquired wealth or considerable pension entitlement (Laczko and Phillipson, 1991).

---

[9]   While all the men in these analyses were in permanent full-time employment at the first interview, only 77% provided information on their gross hourly earnings. Information for the remaining 23% was imputed by constructing a wage model for those with valid wage data and using the coefficients from that model and the explanatory variable values for the men with missing wage data to produce estimates of what these men would have earned.

[10] Similar analyses were not carried out for women because once the female sample had been divided according to the wage distribution the numbers in each subgroup were not sufficient to produce reliable findings.

---

[8]   It is important not to over-stress the importance of this variable, however, as it was only significant at the 10% confidence level.

Female exits from permanent full-time employment

The range of factors that is important in explaining female exits from permanent full-time employment is similar to that for men, but there are some important differences. As for men, age, health problems and owning accommodation outright are the three most important factors associated with female exits from permanent full-time employment. Women are also more likely to exit when they work for smaller establishments and if their partner is unemployed (Table 2.3).

In contrast to men, however, there are also a number of characteristics of female employment that *reduce* the likelihood of women leaving permanent full-time employment. When women report being supervisors or managers at the first interview, their chances of leaving permanent full-time employment are reduced by 32 and 21 percentage points respectively (Table 2.3). Similarly, if they reported receiving job-related training in the four weeks before the first interview their chances of leaving permanent full-time employment by the time of the fifth interview are reduced by 27 percentage points. Thus, it would appear that when women's jobs have positive characteristics, such as managerial or supervisory responsibility or the opportunity to receive training, these characteristics are to some extent able to mitigate the negative effect on participation exerted by factors such as age, health problems and property ownership. The

same variables on job characteristics were included in the male models but were not found to have any effect. Previous literature has not really uncovered these types of positive effect for women and some reasons for this are offered in the conclusion to this chapter.

Summary

This chapter has identified factors associated with movement out of permanent full-time employment by older workers after the age of 50.

Men are more likely to leave full-time employment:

- when they are older compared to when they are younger;
- if they have health problems;
- if they own their home outright;
- if they have been with their employer for a long time (and hence have more chance of having an occupational pension);
- if they have higher qualifications or earnings.

Regional and industrial factors were also important, albeit to a lesser degree. The male analyses were able to identify relatively few factors acting to keep men in permanent full-time employment, but having a partner in paid employment and working in particular sectors (especially health) come into this category.

With the notable exception of health problems, *most of the factors associated with an increased likelihood of exit by men are indicators of advantage in the labour market.* This is especially the case regarding the outright ownership of accommodation, years continuously employed, qualifications and earnings. It was instructive, however, that when models were run separately for low, medium and high earning men, the low earners were particularly likely to exit because of health problems. Overall, and where the LFS contains the range of variables necessary for us to make a comparison, the results of the male analyses are largely consistent with the existing empirical literature on the reasons for declining

Table 2.3: Factors encouraging movement out of permanent full-time employment, women

Factor (measured at first interview)	Percentage impact (%)	Level of statistical significance (%)
Age	+16	1
Health problem	+47	1
Owns accommodation outright	+46	1
Supervisor	−32	1
Establishment size under 25	+84	5
Received job-related training in last four weeks	−27	5
Partner is unemployed	+91	5
Manager	−21	5

employment among older workers. This suggests that the period from 1997 to 2001,[11] while coinciding with a levelling out of the decline in employment rates among older male workers, did not involve any substantial change in the range of factors encouraging this decline.

For women, as with men, age, health problems and the outright ownership of accommodation tended to be positively associated with an increased likelihood of exit from permanent full-time employment. Working for a small establishment and having an unemployed partner also had this effect. But women differed from men in that there were a number of job characteristics, such as managerial or supervisory responsibility or the opportunity to receive training, which were to some extent able to mitigate the negative effect on participation exerted by factors such as age, health problems and property ownership. These same job characteristics were considered in the male models but were not found to have any effect. Similarly, previous empirical research on older workers in the UK labour market has tended not to reach these conclusions. This suggests that the period since 1997, when the employment rate for women aged 50 and above has in fact increased, has been characterised by *a more positive labour market environment for older women*, in which at least those with better jobs have been more inclined to remain in employment than was the case in the recent past.

It was noted at the beginning of this chapter that most exits out of permanent full-time employment were to unemployment or economic inactivity. The next chapter, however, examines the factors that are associated with movements into various types of 'flexible' employment, which some commentators have identified as a possible way for older workers to maintain labour market participation once they have left permanent full-time employment.

---

[11] While our sample entered the LFS between 1997 and 2000, fifth wave data for the latest cohort was collected in 2001.

3

Movements into flexible employment

Introduction

Chapter 2 examined factors associated with movement by older workers out of permanent full-time employment. This chapter identifies the characteristics associated with the particular routes that these people take when they leave such stable jobs. This study takes a particular interest in factors encouraging movement into three types of 'flexible' or non-standard employment: self-employment, temporary employment and part-time employment.[1] This chapter analyses characteristics of those who make transitions of this type, relative to those who move from a full-time job into economic inactivity, which is the most common form of transition underpinning the decline in labour market participation among older workers. There is relatively little previous research on the factors associated with a shift from permanent full-time employment into flexible employment on the part of older workers, so these analyses are exploratory.

As was shown in Chapter 2, about one in eight (12%) of those respondents who were in permanent full-time employment at wave one had moved out of it by wave five (see Table 2.1). It is necessary in the first instance to describe in more detail the different transitions out of permanent full-time employment that were taken by these members of the cohort. Table 3.1 shows the destinations at the fifth interview of men and women who had moved out of permanent full-time employment.

Overall, more than half (56%) of those respondents who had moved out of permanent full-time employment by their fifth interview were not working. Most of these had left the workforce entirely (46%), but a considerable proportion of respondents (10%) had become unemployed.[2] There is a marked contrast between men and women in the proportion of respondents who stopped working as opposed to taking up different kinds of work: more than six in 10 men (62%) compared with just over four in 10 (44%) women. This may partly reflect the fact that men were much more likely than women to be observed in permanent full-time employment at the first interview, so that women may often have already made transitions out of permanent full-time employment before entering the sample.

Table 3.1: Destinations of those who moved out of permanent full-time employment, by gender (%)

Destination	Male	Female	All
Self-employment	12	2	8
Temporary employment	10	7	9
Part-time employment	16	46	26
Unemployment	12	6	10
Economic inactivity	50	38	46
Base	*1,345*	*706*	*2,051*

[1] It is worth noting that information on movements from permanent full-time employment to self-employment, temporary employment or part-time employment is based on self-reporting by the respondents.

[2] The main distinction between unemployment and economic inactivity is that people are classified as unemployed if they are without work but are available for and seeking work but as economically inactive if they are without work and are either not available for work or not seeking work, or both.

Those men who left permanent for flexible employment are spread fairly evenly across the three types, with 12% entering self-employment, 10% temporary employment and 16% part-time employment (Table 3.1). In contrast, female transitions centre very much on exits to part-time employment – a route taken by 46% of women, while only 7% of women entered temporary jobs and only 2% became self-employed.[3]

Econometric models were run to identify the factors encouraging movement into self-employment, temporary employment, or part-time employment, rather than economic inactivity.[4] These models considered a similar range of factors that may influence employment behaviour to those that were considered in the analysis described in Chapter 2 and were run separately for men and women. The main findings of interest are summarised below.[5]

Movements into temporary employment

As described above, 10% of men and 7% of women who had moved out of permanent full-time employment by the fifth interview had made a transition into temporary employment. Table 3.2 highlights the factors most strongly associated

Table 3.2: Factors associated with movements into temporary employment rather than economic inactivity

Factor (measured at first interview)	Men	Women
Years with the current employer	Yes (–)	Yes (–)
Age	Yes (–)	Yes (–)
Health problem	Yes (–)	No
Owns accommodation outright	Yes (–)	No
Higher degree	No	Yes (+)
Partner in paid work	No	Yes (+)
Accommodation is rented	No	Yes (–)
Works in personal and protective services	No	Yes (+)

Note: (+) indicates a positive association and (–) a negative association.

with this type of transition as compared to leaving the workforce.

Four of the factors associated with any kind of move out of a full-time permanent job (see Chapter 2) are also ones that make economic inactivity a more likely outcome than temporary work. A long work record with one's present employer reduced a worker's chance of taking temporary work rather than leaving the workforce. As was argued in Chapter 2, in many cases this may be due to their having accumulated an occupational pension entitlement, which makes it easier to afford to stop working entirely. The same tendency was observed for relatively older workers, those with health problems and those who owned their homes outright.

Of these factors, years with the current employer and age also exert a negative influence on temporary employment for women, but, just as there are some positive factors associated with women remaining in permanent full-time employment, there are also some factors that make it more likely that women would enter temporary work. Women with a higher degree[6] or who worked in personal or protective services at the time of the first interview were more likely

---

[3] Because it was possible for the three categories of flexible employment to overlap, it was necessary to impose a priority rule in order to make the categories mutually exclusive. Thus, the self-employed were classified as self-employed whether they were full-time or part-time: the fact of self-employment was taken to be the salient feature of their employment situation. Any part-time workers who were not self-employed were classified as part-time, even if they were also temporary workers. It is more accurate, therefore, to refer to temporary workers as they appear in these analyses as full-time temporary workers. We continue to refer to them simply as temporary workers for the sake of brevity.

[4] More specifically, multinomial logistic regression models were used for the analyses. The models identified the factors associated with movements into self-employment, temporary employment, part-time employment or unemployment, as opposed to economic inactivity. The analyses regarding movements into unemployment rather than economic inactivity are not reported.

[5] Full statistical results from the analyses used in this chapter are available from the authors on request.

[6] Women with higher degrees who made transitions from permanent full-time to temporary employment tended to be in professional occupations.

to move into temporary employment. So were women whose partners were in paid work at the first interview. Living in rented accommodation rather than owning a property with a mortgage had the reverse effect.

This seems to suggest that women enter temporary work for more positive reasons than men – a hypothesis supported to some extent by analysis of an LFS question on why the respondent was in a temporary job. Whereas 51% of men answered 'because I could not find a permanent job', this was the case for only 40% of women.

Movements into self-employment

As is shown in Table 3.1, men are more likely than women to move out of permanent full-time employment into self-employment (12% against 2% of those who moved out of permanent full-time employment). Table 3.3 identifies the factors associated most strongly with transitions of this type.

Age and health problems are again inhibiting factors discouraging male transitions into an alternative form of work rather than out of the workforce. However, in the case of self-

employment there are also a number of positive factors associated with such transitions for men. Men with dependent children have a greater chance of becoming self-employed rather than giving up work, perhaps suggesting that greater financial responsibilities encourage men to use self-employment to help them through this transition. It tends to be higher earners who became self-employed: higher gross hourly wages are associated with a move to self-employment. So are better qualifications, but having at least NVQ Level 3 (A levels and their vocational equivalents) makes a bigger difference than having degree-level qualifications. The kind of workplace that men leave also plays a role: those from smaller workplaces (1-10 employees) rather than larger ones are more likely to become self-employed, as are those who have worked in the transport and communications industry.[7]

While a model was used to consider female transitions into self-employment, the number of women making this transition was too low to yield any statistically significant effects.

Movements into part-time employment

The final type of movement into 'flexible' employment considered in this chapter is the shift into part-time employment. This pathway is taken by about one in six men (16%) who moved out of permanent full-time jobs and almost half (46%) of women who did likewise. Table 3.4 shows the factors associated most strongly with this shift.

For men, advancing age and health problems reduce the chance of a shift down to part-time employment, rather than leaving work altogether. Thus these two factors are negatively associated with moves to all three forms of 'flexible' employment. More years with the current employer also make a part-time work transition less likely. There are some positive factors, however, that encourage men to take this course. One is having received training in the four weeks prior to the first interview; as in the case of self-employment, working in a small establishment

Table 3.3: Factors associated with movements into self-employment rather than economic inactivity

Factor (measured at first interview)	Men	Women
Age	Yes (–)	No
Health problem	Yes (–)	No
Number of dependent children in household	Yes (+)	No
Number of employees at workplace is 1-10	Yes (+)	No
Gross hourly earnings	Yes (+)	No
Highest qualifications is NVQ3 equivalent	Yes (+)	No
Industry is transport and communication	Yes (+)	No
Occupation is personal and protective services	Yes (–)	No

Note: (+) indicates a positive association and (–) a negative association.

---

[7] In most cases, the respondent remained in the same industry after the transition to self-employment.

Table 3.4: Factors associated with movements into part-time employment rather than economic inactivity

Factor (measured at first interview)	Men	Women
Age	Yes (-)	Yes (-)
Years with the current employer	Yes (-)	No
Received job-related training in last four weeks	Yes (+)	No
Health problem	Yes (-)	Yes (-)
Highest qualifications is NVQ3 equivalent	Yes (+)	No
Number of employees at workplace is 1-10	Yes (+)	No
Lives in Northern Ireland, the North or Scotland	No	Yes (-)
Occupation is elementary	No	Yes (+)
Worked for health authority or NHS Trust hospital	No	Yes (+)
Number of dependent children in household	No	Yes (+)

Note: (+) indicates a positive association and (-) a negative association.

(1-10 employees) and having qualifications at least at NVQ Level 3 have similar effects.

Women are also less likely to enter part-time employment rather than leaving work if they are older or have health problems, but years with the current employer had no measurable effect for them. There was also no training or qualifications effect for women, but instead they were more likely to enter part-time employment if they had been in an elementary occupation[8] at the first interview or worked for a health authority or NHS Trust hospital.

On the whole, it would appear that entry into part-time employment is to some extent associated with labour market advantage on the part of men (training and qualifications) and disadvantage on the part of women (elementary occupation). This suggestion is contradicted, however, by examination of the change in gross hourly wages by gender associated with the transition from permanent full-time to part-time employment. Whereas men experienced a 9% decline in gross hourly earnings (from £9.66 per hour to £8.79 per hour) when making this transition, women experienced a 7% increase (from £6.72 per hour to £7.16). Maintaining labour market participation through part-time employment would appear to be at considerable cost to men, whereas it is to the advantage of women, at least as far as average hourly pay is concerned.[9]

Reduced hours

The final type of transition considered in this chapter involves looking at respondents who remained in permanent full-time employment at the end of the year in question, but who experienced a substantial reduction in the number of hours they usually worked per week. Transitions of this type can be seen as similar in character to those involving movements into flexible employment, as reducing hours in this way might also potentially represent a 'bridge' to retirement.[10]

Table 3.5 shows the pattern of changing hours among respondents who were observed in permanent full-time employment at both the first and fifth interviews.

---

[8] Elementary occupations are those defined by the Standard Occupational Classification as requiring the knowledge and experience necessary to perform mostly routine tasks, often involving the use of simple hand-held tools and, in some cases, requiring a degree of physical effort. They do not require formal educational qualifications but will usually have an associated short period of formal experience-related training. Examples of jobs in this category include cleaner, packer and catering assistant.

[9] Similar comparisons were carried out regarding change in gross hourly earnings for men and women when making the transition from permanent full-time employment to temporary employment, but no interesting findings emerged. Male earnings remained fixed at £8.89 per hour, while female earnings rose marginally from £7.58 per hour to £7.75. Data was not collected on self-employed earnings.

[10] As with the analyses of movement from permanent full-time employment to flexible employment, the key changes involved in these analyses are based on self-reporting. Thus, these analyses are based on respondents who reported that they remained in permanent full-time employment but at the same time reported a drop in their usual weekly hours.

Table 3.5: Change in hours, by gender, among respondents who were in permanent full-time employment at both the first and fifth interviews (%)

Change in usual hours worked per week between first and fifth interviews	Male	Female	All
Increased by 6 hours or more	6	4	6
Increased by 1-5 hours	16	15	16
No change	49	56	51
Reduced by 1-5 hours	21	18	20
Reduced by 6 hours or more	9	6	8
Mean change	-0.55	-0.31	-0.48
Base	*9,860*	*4,390*	*14,250*

On average, there was very little tendency for older workers to change their hours from the first to the fifth quarters. The mean usual hours worked per week fell by about half an hour, with the decline being somewhat greater for men than for women. This average includes 49% of men and 56% of women who did not change their usual hours. On the other hand, quite a large proportion did experience changes. About one in 17 respondents (6%) experienced a substantial increase in hours (of six hours per week or more), while a further one in six (16%) saw increases of between one and five hours (Table 3.5). In contrast, one in five older workers who remained in permanent full-time employment saw a reduction of between one and five hours, while one in 12 (8%) experienced reductions that were greater than this. Men were somewhat more likely than women to experience change (increase or reduction) in the numbers of hours they worked.

There is particular interest in those who have experienced substantial reductions in hours while remaining in permanent full-time employment, since they have experienced a change most similar in character to a transition into flexible employment. In addition, there is less chance with this group that the apparent reduction is simply the result of recall error, which may account for quite a large proportion of those changes that involve differences of only a few hours per week.

With this in mind, the study built a model to consider factors associated with reducing working time by more than five hours a week while staying in a permanent full-time job. Table 3.6 summarises the most important factors that emerged from this analysis.

The models produced some interesting findings. Reductions in hours are less likely the more men earn, but in other ways appear to be strongly associated with an advantaged labour market position at the first interview. For example, reductions in hours for men are more common when the respondent is a manager or professional and has qualifications. The female analyses produced similar findings, with gross hourly earnings having a negative effect on this type of transition but being highly qualified and from a managerial or professional background having a positive effect.

More detailed analysis of the hours actually worked by those who experience a substantial reduction in hours shows that they are typically

Table 3.6: Factors associated with a substantial reduction in weekly hours worked, for those remaining in permanent full-time employment

Factor (measured at first interview)	Men	Women
Gross hourly earnings	Yes (-)	Yes (-)
Industry is transport and communication or other services	Yes (+)	No
Manager	Yes (+)	Yes (+)
Highest qualification is equivalent to NVQ 2-5	Yes (+)	Yes (+)
Occupation is associate professional, clerical or skilled manual	Yes (-)	Yes (-)
Occupation is professional	Yes (+)	Yes (+)
Occupational is sales	Yes (+)	Yes (-)
Occupation is process operative	No	Yes (-)
Works in central or local government	Yes (-)	No
Lives in Scotland or North West	Yes (-)	Yes (-)
Lives in Northern Ireland, West Midlands or North	Yes (-)	No
Partner is unemployed	No	Yes (+)

Note: (+) indicates a positive association and (-) a negative association.

people who worked very long hours at the time of the first interview but have reduced to something more like normal full-time working hours by the fifth interview. Men in this category reduced their hours from an average of 54 per week to 41 per week. The equivalent reduction for women is from 47 hours per week to 34 per week. In the majority of cases, and especially in the case of professionals, this reduction was carried out while remaining in the same broad occupational group. For managers however, there is a greater tendency to switch to a lower grade occupation. Among those who experience a substantial reduction in hours, male managers switched to a lower grade occupation in 11% of cases and women did so in 29% of cases. This occupational downgrading on the part of women often involves switching to administrative and clerical work. In the great majority of cases, however, reducing hours means staying in the same occupational group and maintaining pay levels. In fact, as a similar level of weekly pay is usually combined with a large reduction in hours, those who reduce their hours experience substantial increases in gross hourly pay on average.

Summary

This chapter has identified the factors associated with movement into three types of flexible employment – temporary employment, self-employment and part-time employment – as well as the factors associated with substantial reductions in hours worked per week among older workers who remain in permanent full-time employment.

The two factors most consistently associated with the chances of entering flexible employment compared to leaving work are negative ones. The first is age: the older that people are when they leave full-time permanent employment the less likely they are of making a transition via flexible employment. This is true among men for all the three flexible categories, and among women for temporary and part-time employment. The second is health: people leaving jobs with long-term health problems are less likely to take a part-time job (men and women) or a temporary job (men), or to become self-employed (men).

Other factors applied differentially to various kinds of flexible work for men and for women. One set of characteristics is those associated with positive, financial reasons for leaving work entirely; conversely, those who did not have these characteristics may have needed to take flexible jobs for the 'negative' reason of not being able to afford to retire. People who have spent longer with their employer, and thus are more likely to have sufficient pension income, are less likely to enter temporary work (both men and women), self-employment (men) or part-time work (men). Men who have paid off the mortgage are less likely to do temporary work, while men supporting dependent children are more likely to become self-employed.

A positive reason for being more likely to take flexible jobs is labour market advantage, which can make it easier to find such work. Women with degrees are more likely to get temporary jobs after leaving permanent ones; better-paid and better-trained men are more likely to find part-time work. But it could also work the other way around – women in elementary occupations are more likely to become part-time. Finally, an interesting factor associated with an increased chance of men working part-time or becoming self-employed is having been in a small workplace before leaving full-time permanent work.

Reductions in hours while remaining in permanent full-time employment are less likely the more men earn, but in other ways appear to be strongly associated with an advantaged labour market position at the first interview. For example, reductions in hours for men are more common when the respondent is a manager or professional and has qualifications. The female analyses produced similar findings, with gross hourly earnings having a negative effect on this type of transition but being highly qualified and from a managerial or professional background having a positive effect. In the great majority of cases, *reducing hours* means staying in the same occupational group and maintaining pay levels, often effectively increasing hourly pay.

It was stated at the beginning of this chapter that analyses of the factors associated with a shift from permanent full-time employment to flexible employment are somewhat exploratory, because this specific issue has not been investigated in any detail by the existing empirical literature.

What has emerged is a complex and in some cases contradictory set of findings that do not present a particularly clear picture of the kinds of characteristics that encourage older workers to shift into flexible employment rather than economic inactivity.

Many of the factors revealed by Chapter 2 as making people more likely to leave permanent full-time jobs in the first place were also found to increase the chances of leaving the workforce altogether rather than taking a flexible job. Of consistent importance here are years spent with the current employer, age, health problems and outright ownership of property.

However, there are a number of positive factors that encourage older workers to move into flexible employment rather than economic inactivity, helping to counterbalance the effect of the negative influences referred to above. These tend to vary according to gender and to the type of flexible employment under consideration. For example, men with intermediate-level qualifications and higher pay are more likely to move into self-employment, whereas women with higher degrees are more likely to move into temporary employment. Men with intermediate-level qualifications and recent experience of training are more likely to enter part-time employment, but the same does not apply for women. Men experience a substantial drop in hourly earnings when moving into part-time employment, whereas women enjoyed an increase.

The implications of these findings for the viability of flexible employment as an alternative to economic inactivity and as a potential bridge from permanent full-time employment to retirement are considered in the concluding Chapter 5. First, however, the following chapter considers another aspect of flexible employment that influences how viable a transition method it will be: its quality.

4

Flexible employment: good jobs or bad?

Introduction

As discussed in Chapter 1, there are concerns that the promotion of flexible or 'bridge' jobs as an alternative to leaving the labour market between age 50 and retirement age will result in an age-segmented labour force, with older workers consigned to poor quality and low paying jobs. If such jobs came to substitute for permanent full-time employment, the implications for financial security post-retirement could be significant, with lower earnings being associated with fewer opportunities to save and a reduced likelihood of occupational pensions being available. However, as an alternative to unemployment and economic inactivity the opportunities offered by 'bridge' jobs may be advantageous. While many part-time and temporary jobs are characterised by poor terms and conditions, others are comparable to the average full-time permanent position. Indeed many 'standard' jobs do not escape the poor quality classification (Rubery, 1998). Therefore the extent to which flexible jobs are bad jobs remains unclear.

Job quality

Given the perceived need to encourage older people to consider flexible employment as an alternative to inactivity and indeed the desire among this age group for a more gradual withdrawal from labour force participation (Casey et al, 1991), it is necessary to consider the quality of these jobs. Below we deploy a number of measures to assess the quality of flexible employment in comparison with full-time permanent jobs held by the over 50 age group in our LFS cohort. A good job ideally fulfils criteria such as adequate levels of pay, equitable treatment in terms of access to training, freedom from tight control regimes and security of contract. As well as looking at these aspects, we assess job satisfaction levels, because subjective perceptions are recognised as important in considering how 'good' a job is.

Stability

It could be argued that stability should not be included within the basket of quality measures for older workers. One of the key messages being transmitted from organisations such as the Employers' Forum on Age is that, as workers age, a more wide-ranging set of employment and non-employment alternatives, with ease of movement between them, should be welcomed as normal practice. Therefore, instead of being alarmed at the prospect of employment disjunctures in which individuals leave work, spend a period of semi-retirement, then perhaps combine intermittent paid work with voluntary community activities, these should be embraced as an acceptable course of events. Such movements in and out of or between jobs could represent a twilight career trajectory sensitive to the changing needs of an older workforce whose health may be deteriorating or who, sandwiched between two generations, have caring demands from older and younger relatives.

However, it must be recognised that such practices render employees of any age potentially vulnerable to employers who may take advantage of the lower bargaining power of workers whose links to the workplace have been weakened. They may offer poor terms and conditions on a hire-and-fire basis, over which employees have little control.

Table 4.1 examines how stable different kinds of job are among the 50+ age group by looking at each category of job at first interview (wave one) and considering the chance of different outcomes a year later (wave five). It reveals that part-time employment is less stable than permanent full-time employment. Within this category women are less likely to exit than men: 32% of men and 18% of women exited a part-time position between waves one and five, which contrasts with 15% of permanent full-time employed men and 14% of permanent full-time employed women. Self-employment represents the most stable employment type with just one tenth of men and women leaving this state (although of course instability can exist within self-employment, with ups and downs in the amount of work that one obtains). This finding is consistent with earlier research on labour market transitions after unemployment (Bryson and White, 1996). It reflects the ability of own account workers to control their own hours and activities including the contraction of operations during downturns.

Although temporary contracts are, by definition, less stable, it is of concern that 14% of men and 12% of women in temporary jobs are no longer

working a year later. The probability of transferring into unemployment or inactivity is highest for those on temporary or part-time contracts. There is therefore a degree of vulnerability associated with these temporary and part-time positions. They are not as stable as their permanent full-time equivalents and temporary workers are at greatest risk of transferring to inactivity or unemployment. While temporary and part-time contracts might represent a viable alternative to labour market exit, they may not, for many, offer long-term solutions to the problem of inactivity.

Training opportunities

The LFS asks whether respondents have had any training (either on the job or away from the job) in the past three months. The first row of Table 4.2 indicates that, regardless of age, part-timers are less likely to have received any training. Women uniformly appear to receive more training than men in all age groups and employment categories. As workers age they are decreasingly likely to be offered any work-related training, regardless of whether he or she is a full-time, temporary or part-time employee. This is consistent with the findings of Taylor and Urwin's (2001) analysis of the Spring 1997 LFS

Table 4.1: How stable are flexible jobs compared with permanent full-time jobs among the 50+ age group? (%)

Men

		Change at wave five				
Position at wave one	No change	New full-time job	Other job	Unemployed	Inactive	*N*
Permanent full-time employment	86	4	4	2	4	9,587
Part-time employment	67	9	14	2	9	625
Temporary employment	39	24	23	5	9	501
Self-employment	90	4	2	1	4	3,024

Women

		Change at wave five				
Position at wave one	No change	New full-time job	Other job	Unemployed	Inactive	*N*
Permanent full-time employment	85	3	7	1	4	4,160
Part-time employment	82	4	7	1	7	3,857
Temporary employment	44	13	31	3	9	465
Self-employment	88	1	4	1	6	823

Table 4.2: Workers who have undergone training in the previous three months (%)

	Full-time		Temporary		Part-time	
	All	**New**[a]	**All**	**New**[a]	**All**	**New**[a]
All men and women (30+)	15	26	17	28	12	23
Men aged 30-39	16	26	16	27	17	21
Women aged 30-39	20	32	27	41	15	26
Men aged 40-49	15	22	14	22	11	19
Women aged 40-49	19	32	23	43	13	25
Men aged 50+	9	15	9	15	6	14
Women aged 50+	15	25	18	26	8	17

Note: [a] New recruits have been in their current job for less than one year.

cohort, which suggests that the disadvantaged position of older workers with regard to training has not changed markedly from the mid-1990s to the late 1990s and early 2000s (when our cohort was drawn). Focusing on the 50+ age group it is clearly the case that part-time women workers receive far fewer offers of training than their full-time counterparts (whether permanent or temporary). This could be interpreted in a number of ways:

- The work is more likely to be menial and therefore training is not required. This would indicate a lower quality job.
- Employers are less committed to their part-time staff and deny them the training opportunities that might permit progress within the organisation.
- Older workers already have plenty of experience with the sort of work they are undertaking and therefore simply do not need to be trained.
- Older workers do not want to undertake any training.

Therefore, as a single measure, this variable does not define a 'bad' job but can be taken as a warning sign of poorer terms and conditions among part-time work more generally.

The relationship between flexible employment and training was explored in more detail through the use of econometric analyses[1] (the results of

these are presented in Table A.1, in the Appendix). Our main interest is in the probability of training associated with being in one of the flexible employment categories rather than permanent or full-time employment. The models control for the effect of health, occupation, human capital, employment sector (public versus private) and age, and so enable us to measure more precisely the separate impact of being in flexible employment on likelihood of training receipt. The sample is restricted to those who have been employed in their current organisation for less than one year. As new recruits their need for some form of training will be greater than more established employees, for whom training will be related to career progression.

Working in the public sector is associated with a greater likelihood of training among both men and women over 50, but as they age the probability of training decreases. Highly educated men and women in their fifties are the most likely among all educational attainment groups to receive training within a year of starting a new job.

Being in flexible employment is not a significant determinant of training among men over 50. Among older women, flexible employment is associated with training uptake differentials. Women working in part-time, casual temporary and agency temporary employment all experience a lower incidence of training compared with women working full-time or in

---

[1] More specifically, these were binary logistic regression models in which the dependent variable, received training in the past three months, took the value of 0 if no training had been received and 1 if training had been undertaken.

permanent jobs.[2] As this negative impact of flexible employment on training is measured after controlling for the effect of other job and socioeconomic characteristics, it provides convincing evidence of the relatively poor quality of part-time and temporary jobs for older women.

Table 4.3 indicates that the majority of part-time and temporary workers who did not take any training were also not offered any training opportunities. The figures compare unfavourably with full-time permanent staff who did not train; less than half the women and roughly half the men were not offered training. This finding is consistent with Taylor and Urwin (2001) and further underlines the job quality problems of part-time and temporary work in relation to training.[3]

Table 4.3: Employment status by whether training offered (% of respondents *never offered* education or training)

	Full-time permanent	Full-time temporary	Part-time
All men	49	70	71
All women	43	61	59
Men over 49	52	74	68
Women over 49	44	62	59

Sample: Those not taking any job related training in previous three months.

Earnings

The level of earnings is perhaps the most commonly used measure of job quality (Lissenburgh, 2001). The figures presented in Tables 4.4 and 4.5 represent gross hourly pay. The two tables are derived from different data sources, as the LFS does not collect earnings data

from the self-employed. The WiB survey[4] was used as an alternative to compare the earnings of full-time, part-time, temporary and self-employed workers. Looking initially at Table 4.4, based on the LFS, earnings peak for men between the ages of 40 and 49. For women, earnings peak between 30 and 39. For both men and women, hourly pay levels begin to tail off after the age of 50. For those aged 50 and above, full-time permanent employees earn the highest hourly rates, followed by full-time temporary staff. Part-time workers fare worst in terms of hourly rates and there is clearly a wage disadvantage associated with part-time employment contracts. This means that part-time workers are doubly

Table 4.4: Gross hourly pay (£) – are part-time and temporary staff disadvantaged?

	Mean	N
Men		
30-39	9.67	9,040
40-49	10.32	8,115
50+	9.31	7,512
Men 50+		
Full-time permanent	9.51	6,669
Full-time temporary	8.94	242
Part-time	7.25	596
Part-time permanent	6.70	461
Part-time temporary	9.14	135
Women		
30-39	7.44	9,031
40-49	7.21	8,715
50+	6.72	6,421
Women 50+		
Full-time permanent	7.68	3,134
Part-time temporary	7.23	99
Part-time	5.76	3,187
Part-time permanent	5.66	2,966
Part-time temporary	6.99	221

Source: Labour Force Survey (2000)

---

[2] Where respondents report that they are in temporary employment, the LFS asks them to say whether this is casual, is with an employment agency or is fixed-term.

[3] Self-employed workers were not asked about training receipt.

[4] WiB is a nationally representative survey of 2,500 workers aged 20-60 carried out in 2000. Of the respondents, 334 (14%) are self-employed. The interviews were of one-hour duration and included a self-completion component. The survey was designed by a team of researchers from the Policy Studies Institute (Michael White and Deborah Smeaton) and the London School of Economics and Political Science (Steve Hill, Pat McGovern and Colin Mills). It was funded by the ESRC under the phase I 'Future of work' programme.

Table 4.5: Gross hourly pay (£) – part-time, self-employed and temporary workers

Age and status	Mean	N
Employee earnings		
30-39	8.89	548
40-49	9.25	429
50-60	8.62	361
Self-employed earnings		
30-39	13.61	52
40-49	12.76	75
50-60	10.55	58
Men and women aged 50-60		
Full-time permanent	9.40	252
Full-time temporary	9.19	12
Part-time	6.51	94
Self-employed	10.55	58

Source: WiB survey (2000)

disadvantaged financially; they earn less due to reduced hours and they earn less per hour worked.

Table 4.5 presents data on gross hourly pay from the WiB dataset. With just 334 self-employed respondents the results are not as robust as for larger samples, therefore all results pool men and women. For all age groups the self-employed earn more than employees. Focusing on men and women aged 50-60, the self-employed are typically the higher earners, followed by full-time employees, with part-timers firmly at the bottom.

Part-timers aged 50 and above have gross earnings of £6.51 per hour, which is only 69% of permanent employees' hourly wage. This data suggests that self-employed workers benefit financially from their 'flexible' status. It is likely, however, that the characteristics of self-employed workers will differ from those of other groups (Bryson and White, 1996), and it is therefore worthwhile to investigate in more detail any potential earnings advantage they may have by controlling for other factors that might influence pay levels.

Table A.2 shows the results of econometric analyses of the relationship between earnings and employment status, based on the WiB

dataset.[5] The analyses estimated the impact of employment type on pay, while controlling for the effect of qualifications, occupation, gender, age, employment discontinuity, length of service with the current employer and use of computers. As well as distinguishing between self-employment, full-time employment and part-time employment, the analyses made a distinction between different types of self-employment: professional or limited business owner, own account worker without employees, sub-contractor and freelancer.

Own account workers without employees, sub-contractors (the majority of whom have no employees) and employees all earned significantly less than self-employed professional and limited business owners. Given the heterogeneity of self-employed workers it is clearly important to disaggregate wherever possible in order to avoid misleading conclusions based on the conflation of quite distinct labour market positions. As these analyses make clear, the higher average pay of self-employed workers as indicated by Table 4.5 has more to do with the higher earnings of a particular sub-group of the self-employed – employed professional and limited business owners – rather than with any higher earning power on the part of self-employed workers as a whole.

Similar wage models were produced using our LFS cohort (the details of these models are presented in Table A.3). The advantage of the LFS analyses are that sample sizes are large enough to run separate models for those aged 50 and above and to produce separate results for older men and older women. These models again investigated the relationship between gross hourly earnings and employment status, while controlling for a number of other factors that we hypothesised would influence pay. These included years with the current employer, health, age, qualifications, sector, industry and marital status. In comparing different types of

---

[5] More specifically, the analyses are based on an Ordinary Least Squares (OLS) model, which is the appropriate regression technique to use when the variable to be explained (in this case gross hourly earnings) is continuous. The number of workers aged 50 and above in the dataset was not large enough to run a separate regression model for this group, so the model was run on all in employment with controls for age.

employment we are able to distinguish between permanent and full-time employment on the one hand and part-time and temporary employment on the other. We are able to break temporary employment down into fixed-term, casual or agency employment, but do not, of course, have information available on self-employed earnings.

The results in Table A.3 show that human capital, in the form of qualifications, industrial sector, employment tenure and health problems, does exert the expected effects on pay. Longer tenure boosts earnings while ill-health depresses them. Among men aged 50 and above, working in the public sector is associated with lower earnings but for women in the same age group earnings are better in the public sector. The results on the variable of interest – employment type – differ slightly for men and women aged 50 and above. Female part-timers earn 83p less per hour than female full-timers. This is consistent with Lissenburgh's (1996) findings for a representative sample of the population as whole. However, no significant differences were observed among older men. It cannot, therefore, be concluded that part-time work is inferior for men on this measure. Both men and women earned significantly higher wages working on fixed-term temporary contracts compared with permanent employment. This is linked to the fact that, whereas only just over half of all temporary workers were on fixed-term contracts, about 70% of managers and professionals in temporary employment were on fixed-term contracts. No

significant differences among the earnings of older permanent and casual or agency temps could be discerned.

Overall, the relationship between flexible employment and earnings as revealed by the analyses in this section is shown to be complex. Particular types of self-employment (professional and limited business owners), and of temporary employment (fixed-term contracts), are shown to pay better than permanent or full-time employment. While the higher earnings in these types of employment might to some extent be compensation for the greater degree of risk associated with them compared to permanent full-time employment, this higher pay can be seen as a general indicator of greater job quality. In contrast, part-time employment, at least for women, is shown to be relatively low paying and, according to this measure therefore, as inferior in quality to full-time work.

Job satisfaction

Figure 4.1 uses the WiB data to differentiate between different types of employment according to overall levels of job satisfaction. It is assumed that this overall measure balances satisfaction with various components of work such as pay, hours, workload and scope to use abilities. Among men aged 50 and above, part-timers are the least likely to be completely or

Figure 4.1: Proportion of the 50+ age group 'completely' or 'very' satisfied with their job overall (%)

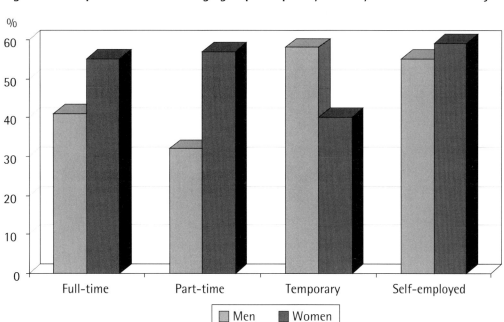

very satisfied (32%), while those employed on a temporary contract are the most satisfied (58%). The reverse applies to women, with temporary workers the least satisfied (40%). Examination of individual job attributes reveals few significant differences between satisfaction levels and employment type, with the exception of workload among women and use of skills among men. Female temporary workers are significantly more likely to be dissatisfied with the amount of work that they are expected to perform. If the workload carried by female temporary workers is more than, or even the same as, their permanent counterparts it is likely that resentment will build up, as long-term rewards for such endeavours do not exist. However, it is not clear why male temporary workers do not report the same depressed levels of satisfaction. Among men aged 50 and above, both part-time and temporary employees are significantly less satisfied than the self-employed and permanent full-time workers, with their opportunity to exploit skills and abilities accumulated over the years. This is an important component of work for both men and women, cited more frequently than any other facet of work as 'essential' or 'very important'. Therefore, manipulation of levels of pay associated with employment types (particularly part-time work) will only go so far in rendering a job attractive. The intrinsic dimensions of a job, such as autonomy, a sense of achievement and use of skills, are often just as, if not more, important than the extrinsic rewards of work such as pay and benefits. Hence, self-employment is invariably associated with enhanced levels of job satisfaction.

Supervisory or labour process control

The ability to take a brief break of 10 minutes duration without seeking permission is widely available throughout the occupational spectrum. However, roughly a quarter of all employees are denied this entitlement and must first gain authorisation from a supervisor or line manager. Such levels of control may reflect the nature of the work task; examples include frontline customer service jobs such as supermarket checkout operators and telephone call centre personnel, or other jobs from assembly-line workers to air traffic control staff. Control may also be applied primarily to extract the maximum

work effort from staff, thereby avoiding loss of profit. For many, freedom from overbearing task and time control is an important feature of their job and is one of the main motivations for shifting to self-employment for men and women alike. Therefore, the ability to take a short break at will is included in the selection of job quality measures. Is there an association between extreme levels of supervisory/labour process control and employment type?

Econometric analyses were carried out to investigate the factors associated with not being allowed to take a 10-minute break without prior permission.[6] Control variables in this analysis included time with the current employer, sector, age, class, union presence, industry and gender. The results are derived using the WiB dataset. Due to the smaller sample size of this survey, models disaggregating by age were not possible. Inclusion of an age variable indicates that men are significantly less likely to be denied the freedom to take a break at will as they get older. However, this finding is not significant for women. Women are less likely than men to be free from close supervisory or labour process control. The presence of a trade union in the workplace and, for men, working in the public sector, means that employees are more likely to be denied the freedom of a 10-minute break. For both men and women, working in a lower non-manual or manual occupation is significantly associated with a greater likelihood of being denied the freedom to independently choose to take a break.

In terms of employment type the only significant differences, having controlled for other factors affecting time sovereignty, apply to women. Part-time and casual temporary women workers are more likely to be denied freedom to take a break at will. The increased levels of control associated with such contracts may be taken as an indicator of inferior working conditions.

---

[6] More specifically, a binary logistic regression model was produced, in which the dependent variable took the value of 0 if a break was allowed and 1 if a break was not allowed without prior permission.

Table 4.6: Quality chart: relative to full-time permanent jobs among the 50+

Men

	Stability	Training	Earnings	Satisfaction	Time autonomy
Part-time	–	–	O	–	O
Temporary	–	+	+[a]	+	O
Self-employed	+	–	i/+[b]	+	+

Women

	Stability	Training	Earnings	Satisfaction	Time autonomy
Part-time	– (slight)	–	–	+	–
Temporary	–	+	+[a]	–	–[c]
Self-employed	+	–	O/+[b]	+	+

Notes: + indicates a positive association, – a negative association and O no difference.

[a] Fixed-term contract temps only.

[b] Significantly superior earnings only associated with professional practice and limited business self employed.

[c] Casual temps only.

Summary

Comparing men and women and the various employment types, a varied picture emerges. Compared with full-time permanent employment the flexible alternatives are less advantageous according to some measures but superior on others. These differences are presented in summary form in Table 4.6.

Part-time work among men is characterised by depressed security, training uptake and satisfaction levels, although no significant differences exist in terms of earnings and levels of control. Women working part-time differ from men, with higher levels of satisfaction expressed when compared with their full-time counterparts aged 50 and above, and with almost the same levels of job security as women working full-time. However, their earnings are lower and they are less likely to enjoy freedom from tight supervisory control. Therefore, it can be concluded, with a few exceptions, that part-time work is inferior to full-time employment for both men and women.

Temporary contracts differ according to whether they are of the fixed-term, casual or agency variety. Among older women temporary contracts do offer training opportunities, but this may be inevitable, as, by definition, these women are more likely to be new to the job and require, at a minimum, some induction training. Fixed-term contracts offer higher earnings, while casual temporary employees work under tighter control regimes. Overall, women exhibit high levels of dissatisfaction with temporary working arrangements; in contrast, male temporary workers are more satisfied than male permanent workers among those aged 50 and above. It is possible that these men are performing their old jobs under a new contractual arrangement in order to access their pensions and are entirely content with the new employment relationship. They receive more training and, among the fixed-term workers, earn higher salaries. Temporary contracts among older men cannot, on the whole, be dismissed as inferior to permanent jobs. However, it is of concern that exits from temporary jobs are more likely than any other type of job exit to lead to unemployment and inactivity rather than another job. Their shorter duration therefore remains problematic for some.

Most of the self-employed men and women do not have a significantly different earnings profile compared with employees, although they do enjoy the possibility, if successful, of far higher earnings. Professional practice and limited business ownership, for example, is associated with enhanced levels of earnings. Training is a problem for the self-employed, who often complain that they have neither the time nor the resources for self-development or further skill acquisition (Cohen and Mallon, 1999). As a consequence, self-employed workers are far less likely than full-time employees to have received any training (Smeaton, 1992).[7] Self-employed workers appear to enjoy greater security in terms of employment tenure. However, this simple measure conceals the potential for periods of extreme hardship as they are vulnerable to economic vicissitudes to which they may respond by contracting operations, depleting savings and enduring periods of underemployment; longer tenure[8] may represent survival at a cost. Despite such potential problems both self-employed men and women consistently report greater satisfaction with their jobs. Of the three types of flexible employment considered in this chapter, self-employment appears to offer quality comparable, on average, with full-time permanent employee opportunities. There are of course pitfalls and not all will succeed. Nevertheless, satisfaction levels cannot be discounted, and self-employment provides a range of opportunities and benefits that are perceived as superior to the average employee position.

---

[7] Training for the self-employed was not considered in this chapter's analyses due to data constraints, so these conclusions are derived from earlier research.

[8] It should be noted that self-employment tenure figures, derived from cross-sectional surveys, can be misleading. They reflect the longevity of successful businesses, that is those that have not failed. Failure rates among the first few years of a new business are very high and this vulnerability is not captured in the 'quality' table above. This is a distinct weakness.

5

Conclusions and policy implications

Conclusions

This report has addressed three main issues:

- What factors are associated with exits from permanent full-time employment among men and women aged between 50 and state pension age?
- What factors are associated with movements from permanent full-time employment to flexible employment for this group of older workers?
- How good is flexible employment relative to permanent full-time employment?

While it is not necessary to repeat in detail the main findings from the research, which are described at length in the preceding chapters, it is useful to recap on the key results before drawing out more general conclusions from the study.

Factors associated with exits from permanent full-time employment

The factors associated with exit from permanent full-time employment among men are redolent of the 'two nations' in early retirement notion familiar in this field of research. On the one hand, certain advantages appear to enable some people to leave work as a positive choice. Workers over 50 are more likely to leave jobs if they have been with their present employer for longer and therefore more likely to have accumulated savings and pension entitlements. So are those who have paid off their mortgages. On the other hand, people are more likely to leave full-time jobs if they have health problems, especially low-paid men. For this group, 'early

retirement' is more likely to be the result of an inability to stay in employment, rather than a positive choice to leave it. The most important factor of all in explaining male exits from permanent full-time employment, however, is age, with the likelihood of exit increasing as the state pension age draws near. While we do not have the data to test whether this is due to age discrimination, it is certainly consistent with that interpretation.

Advancing age is also the factor associated most strongly with an increased likelihood of exit from permanent full-time employment among older women. As with men, health problems and the outright ownership of property are also important. Unlike men, however, older women are also more likely to stay in permanent full-time employment if they are in relatively good jobs. Women who are managers, supervisors or have recently received job-related training are less likely to leave their jobs. While this may be evidence of a more positive labour market environment for older women, whose employment rates have actually increased since 1997, it may also reflect the weaker influence for women of the wealth-related factors that play a role in encouraging men to leave work. Years with the current employer have no effect on women's exit probability, for example, which may reflect women's less substantial occupational pension entitlements.

The factors associated with movement into flexible employment

Many of the factors most strongly associated with leaving a permanent full-time job also make it more likely that people will leave work altogether rather than obtain flexible employment. Of consistent importance here are years spent with the current employer, age, health problems and outright ownership of property.

However, there are a number of positive factors that encourage older workers to move into flexible employment rather than leaving the workforce, but these tend to vary according to gender and to the type of flexible employment under consideration. For example, men with intermediate-level qualifications and higher pay are more likely to move into self-employment, whereas women with higher degrees are more likely to move into temporary employment. Men with intermediate-level qualifications and recent experience of training are more likely to enter part-time employment, but the same did not apply to women. Reductions in hours while remaining in permanent full-time employment are more common for managers and professionals and among those with qualifications. This is true for both men and women.

The quality of flexible employment

Measured against the yardstick of permanent full-time employment, the quality of flexible employment was found to vary according to the type of flexible employment under consideration. There is also a substantial amount of variation in quality *within* particular categories of flexible employment.

Self-employment offers job quality most comparable to that enjoyed by permanent full-time employees. It was shown to be relatively stable, and the self-employed reported high levels of job satisfaction and had high levels of control over how they spent their time. However, only the more advantaged self-employed workers (those who were professionals or owners of limited businesses) have earnings profiles that are superior to those of permanent full-time employees.

Temporary employment rates next in terms of job quality. As one might expect, it is less stable than permanent full-time employment, but temporary workers are more likely to receive training. As with self-employment, however, earning potential in temporary employment varies substantially according to the type of work under consideration. Whereas those on fixed-

term contracts earn more than comparable permanent full-time employees, this is not the case for casual or agency temporary workers. Again, these workers on fixed-term contracts are more likely to be managers or professionals.

Part-time employment offers the poorest job quality among the three types of flexible employment, especially regarding stability and training opportunities in which it is inferior to permanent full-time employment for both men and women.

Two nations in flexible employment?

Evidence has already been presented to suggest that 'two nations' in early retirement is to some degree an accurate description – especially for older men – of the different routes out of permanent full-time employment taken by those at the higher and lower echelons of the wage distribution. Similar conclusions apply with regard to flexible employment, in that older workers from a more advantaged background are more likely to enter flexible employment rather than leaving the workforce on departure from permanent full-time employment and are especially more likely to enter better quality flexible employment.

Thus, men are more likely to enter self-employment if they have intermediate-level qualifications and higher pay; more likely to enter part-time employment if they have intermediate-level qualifications and training; and more likely to experience reduced hours in permanent full-time work if they are managers or professionals. Women with higher degrees are more likely to enter temporary employment and, like men, are more likely to experience reduced hours in permanent full-time work if they are managers or professionals.

Enjoying better quality flexible employment is particularly dependent on labour market background. Self-employed professionals or limited business owners and managers or professionals on fixed-term contracts are the only flexible workers who earn more than comparable permanent full-time employees. For less advantaged workers in flexible employment, the experience is much more variable and the quality of employment is often poor. This is particularly true of part-time employment, in which older women continue to earn less than comparable full-timers despite the introduction of the Part-time Workers (Prevention of Less Favourable Treatment) Regulations in 2000.

The importance of gender differences

Another general conclusion to be drawn from the study relates to the importance of gender differences on older workers' experiences of employment transitions. Being in better jobs, such as managers and supervisors, and jobs in which training was provided appears to encourage women to *remain* in permanent full-time employment in a way in which it does not for men. Following exit from permanent full-time employment, a majority of older women (compared to a minority of older men) are able to access flexible employment and therefore remain in work. There are often positive characteristics associated with their entry into flexible employment, such as higher degrees being associated with a movement into temporary employment. For men, there are fewer cases of these positive factors and more of negative ones. In particular, men who are less likely to be able to afford to retire – because they have dependent children, have not paid off their mortgage or have not been with an employer long enough to build up sufficient pension – appear more likely to take 'bridge' jobs. However, men who have been trained recently and who are better paid do have a higher than average chance of becoming part-time.

When one considers the *quality* of flexible employment, however, gender differences remain important but tell more of a story of male than female advantage. Older women are far more likely than older men to enter part-time work (which offers the poorest quality of flexible employment), whereas men are more likely to enter self-employment (which offers the best quality). Among entrants to temporary work, men are over-represented among those on fixed-term contracts, at the higher quality end of temporary employment, whereas women are over-represented in casual work, at the lower quality end. The fact that having a higher degree is associated with moving into temporary work for women (usually through fixed-term contracts) while at the same time women are over-represented in casual labour suggests that the 'two nations' in flexible employment

characterisation applies as much to older women as to older men.

In short, women appear more successful than men in finding 'bridge' jobs for positive reasons, but often find that these jobs are of poor quality.

Policy implications

This study has produced a comprehensive but complex series of findings, which cannot be translated into any straightforward set of policy recommendations. It is possible, however, to provide some answers to three broad policy questions.

What can be done to promote the maintenance of older workers in permanent full-time employment?

Workers aged between 50 and state pension age are more likely to leave permanent full-time employment if they are older, have health problems, have been with their current employer for a long time and if they own their home outright. These factors are particularly important for men. There are a number of policy initiatives that can potentially promote the maintenance of older workers in permanent full-time employment when they have these characteristics, but in other respects there are policy gaps that need to be filled.

While the New Deal for Disabled People seeks to encourage sick or disabled people to re-enter work when they are out of the labour market, of more relevance to this discussion are policies that help people with health problems to *remain* in work. Examples of such policies are the job retention and rehabilitation pilots, developed by the Department for Education and Skills. These initiatives target people who are in work but have a health problem and aim to prevent people from losing their jobs either by organising early medical intervention or by reorganising employment to minimise the consequences of the health problem for work performance. While such initiatives are at an early stage of development, our findings on the negative effects of health problems on likelihood of staying in permanent full-time employment suggest that they have a potentially important role.

The fact that the chances of leaving permanent full-time employment increase with age, even after controlling for a wide range of other factors, does not provide direct evidence of age discrimination but is certainly consistent with it. The government is currently seeking to tackle age discrimination through the non-statutory Code of Practice on Age Diversity in Employment, but with the adoption by the European Council of Ministers of the Employment Directive on Equal Treatment, this is due to be fortified by a legislative approach. Specifically, the government is due to introduce antidiscrimination legislation relating to age by 2006. While attempts to outlaw age discrimination have met with difficulties (Epstein, 1999), there is at least the potential that such policies would reduce the number of older workers making exits from permanent full-time employment.

It is less clear how policy could deal with the effects of employment tenure and property ownership on the likelihood of exit. To the extent that employment tenure is a proxy for occupational pension entitlement, the income and wealth effects implied by these factors help older workers to finance their exit from permanent full-time employment before state pension age. Clearly it does not make sense to try to dissuade people from providing for their retirement or paying off their mortgage – to worsen their financial position in order to persuade them to stay in work. However, it is worth considering whether some people retiring early because they think they are well provided for are justified in this belief and, if they are not, looking for ways of creating better information. This point needs to be considered in conjunction with other research findings from the Joseph Rowntree Foundation's 'Transitions after 50' programme.

The study found that older women are less likely to leave permanent full-time employment if they are in relatively good jobs. As such, the adoption or improvement by employers of equal opportunities policies, designed to advance women's relative position in the workplace, are likely to increase employment retention.

What can be done to encourage older workers to move into flexible employment?

While this is not universally the case, there is a strong overall tendency for older workers who move out of permanent full-time employment to move into flexible employment rather than leaving work if they have relatively high levels of human capital and have enjoyed a relatively good permanent full-time job. Therefore, policies designed to improve the human capital of older workers and to help them maintain their position in the occupational hierarchy are likely to encourage them to enter flexible employment as a bridge to retirement, rather than moving out of the workforce.

Among current government policies, New Deal 50 Plus offers an Employment Credit to boost pay and an in-work training grant to help boost human capital, but this programme is only available to older people who have been out of work and claiming benefits for at least six months. This research suggests that similar initiatives might be effective if made available to older people who remain in work. While older workers will of course benefit from the Working Tax Credit, which will boost take-home pay for those on lower wages, there is an argument that this should be available on a more generous basis to older workers. This is because they have a relatively high probability of exiting work compared to younger workers, with all that follows in terms of lost tax revenues and, in many cases, additional benefit payments. If a more generous Working Tax Credit for older people could reduce the employment rate differential between older and younger workers, it would be at least partly self-financing. Policies to encourage employment retention and advancement for people already in work have become an important feature of employment policy in many US states, and older workers in the UK, according to the findings of this research, would be likely to benefit from similar initiatives. The importance of training in encouraging older workers to enter some categories of flexible employment also suggests that the lifelong learning and active ageing agendas continue to be relevant and likely to yield positive results if pursued effectively.

What can be done to improve the quality of flexible employment?

According to a range of measures, self-employment offers the best job quality among the different categories of flexible employment, followed by temporary employment and then part-time employment. There are clearly caveats attached to this concerning the high levels of risk attached to self-employment and the inherent instability of temporary employment. There are also quite large differences *within* types of flexible employment, for example between professionals and limited business owners as opposed to other categories of self-employment, and between temporary workers on fixed-term contracts as opposed to casual or agency workers. The analyses suggest that the greatest shortfalls in job quality are found among casual and agency temporary work and in part-time work as a whole. Policies to improve the quality of flexible employment for older workers would be most effective, therefore, if focused specifically on these categories.

The EU Directive on Fixed Term Contracts and the UK government's response – the proposed Fixed Term Employees (prevention of Less Favourable Treatment) Regulations – seek to regulate employment on fixed-term contracts so as to improve levels of job security and the quality of fixed-term contract work more generally. This research suggests that, at least as far as older workers are concerned, this type of temporary work is less in need of improvement in these respects than other types of temporary work. Given the delay in the EU Directive on Temporary Agency Work, it has been argued by organisations such as the Trades Union Congress that the UK government should take a more proactive approach and extend the employment protection proposed for those on fixed-term contracts to all categories of temporary worker. In doing this, the government would clearly need to have regard to the possible negative impact such regulation might have upon employers' willingness to provide temporary jobs, and further research is required on this. An alternative approach likely to yield some degree of success would be to boost the human capital and earning capacity of older workers more generally, as suggested above, because this in itself would be likely to have some positive impact on the quality of flexible employment.

As noted previously, the introduction of the Part-time Workers (Prevention of Less Favourable Treatment) Regulations in 2000 appears to have had little impact on the earnings of female part-time older workers, since they continue to earn less than comparable female full-timers. This situation may improve once the regulations have had longer to register an impact. In the meantime, it may be that policies such as uprating the National Minimum Wage would be of more benefit for older workers in part-time jobs, since they would benefit disproportionately from such action.

This discussion of policy implications has covered a range of initiatives that have the potential to influence employment in ways that would be of benefit to older workers. However, the heterogeneity of older workers, evidence of which has come through strongly in this research, suggests that a 'one size fits all policy' is not appropriate. Rather, nuanced and sensitive policy interventions are required to sustain employment among older workers while at the same time facilitating their movement towards a fulfilling retirement. Flexible employment can play a bridging role between permanent full-time employment and retirement, but a supportive policy framework is required to ensure it acts to the benefit of older workers, whatever their diverse characteristics.

References

Arrowsmith, J. and McGoldrick, A. (1996) *Breaking the barriers: A survey of managers' attitudes to age and employment*, London: Institute of Management.

Bardasi, R. and Jenkins, S. (2002) *Income in later life: Work history matters*, Bristol/York: The Policy Press/Joseph Rowntree Foundation.

Beck, U. (1992) *Risk society: Towards a new modernity*, London: Sage Publications.

Blundell, R. and Johnson, P. (1998) 'Pensions and labour market participations', *American Economic Review*, vol 88, no 2, pp 168-72.

Blundell, R. and Johnson, P. (1999) 'Pensions and retirement in the UK', in J. Gruber and D. Wise (eds) *Social security and retirement around the world: Volume 1*, Chicago, IL and London: Chicago University Press.

Blundell, R., Meghir, C. and Smith, S. (2000) 'Pension incentives and the pattern of incentives in the UK', in J. Gruber and D. Wise (eds) *Social security and retirement around the world: Volume 2*, Chicago, IL and London: Chicago University Press.

Blundell, R., Meghir, C. and Smith, S. (2001) 'Pension incentives and the pattern of early retirement', *Economic Journal*, vol 112, no 478, pp C153-C170.

Bryson, A. and White, M. (1996) *Moving in and out of self-employment*, London: Policy Studies Institute.

Campbell, N. (1999) *The decline of employment among older people in Britain*, CASE Paper, London: Centre for Analysis of Social Exclusion, London School of Economics and Political Science.

Casey, B. (1991) 'Survey evidence on trends in non standard employment', in A. Pollert (ed) *Farewell to flexibility*, Oxford: Blackwell Publishers.

Casey, B. (1998) *Incentives and disincentives to early and late retirement*, Paris: OECD.

Casey, B. and Wood, S. (1994) 'Great Britain: firm policy, state policy and the employment of older workers', in F. Naschold and B. de Vroom (eds) *Regulating employment and welfare: Company and national policies of labour force participation at the end of the worklife in industrial countries*, Berlin: Walter de Gruyter.

Casey, B., Lakey, J. and Fogarty, M (1991) *The experience and attitudes of older people to work and retirement: Report to the Carnegie Trust Inquiry into the Third Age*, London: Policy Studies Institute.

Cohen, L. and Mallon, M. (1999) 'The transition from organisational employment to portfolio work: perceptions of boundarylessness', *Work, Employment & Society*, vol 13, no 2, pp 329-52.

Dex, S. and McCulloch, A. (1997) *Flexible employment*, Basingstoke: Macmillan.

Dex, S., Lissenburgh, S. and Taylor, M. (1994) *Women and low pay: Identifying the issues*, Equal Opportunities Commission Research Discussion Series No 9, Manchester: Equal Opportunities Commission.

Disney, R. (1996) *Can we afford to grow older?*, Cambridge, MA: MIT Press.

Disney, R. (1999) 'Why have older men stopped working?', in P. Gregg and J. Wadsworth (eds) *The state of working Britain*, Manchester: Manchester University Press, pp 58-74.

Disney, R., Grundy, E. and Johnson, P. (eds) (1997) *The dynamics of retirement: Analyses of the retirement surveys*, DSS Research Report No 72, London: The Stationery Office.

Disney, R., Meghir, C. and Whitehouse, E. (1994) 'Retirement behaviour in Britain', *Fiscal Studies*, vol 15, no 1, pp 24-43.

Doeringer, P. and Piore, M. (1971) *Internal labor markets and manpower Analysis*, Lexington, MA: DC Heath.

Dorsett, R. (2001) *Workless couples: Modelling labour market transitions*, Employment Service Research Report ESR98, Sheffield: Employment Service.

Epstein, R. (1999) 'Age discrimination and employment law', *New Zealand Business Roundtable*, August.

Gallie, D., White, M., Cheng, Y. and Tomlinson, M. (1998) *Restructuring the employment relationship*, Oxford: Oxford University Press.

Hayward, B., Taylor, S., Smith, N. and Davies, G. (1997) *Evaluation of the Campaign for Older Workers*, London: The Stationery Office.

Hutton, W. (1995) *The state we're in*, London: Jonathan Cape.

Kalleberg, A., Reskin, B. and Hudson, K. (2000) 'Bad jobs in America: standard and nonstandard employment relations and job quality in the United States', *American Sociological Review*, vol 65, pp 256-78.

Laczko, F. and Phillipson, C. (1991) *Changing work and retirement: Social policy and the older worker*, Milton Keynes: Open University Press.

Lissenburgh, S. (1996) *Value for money: The costs and benefits of giving part-time workers equal rights*, London: Trades Union Congress.

Lissenburgh, S. (2001) *New Deal for the Long Term Unemployed pilots: Quantitative evaluation using stage 2 survey*, Employment Service Research Report ESR81, Sheffield: Employment Service.

Machin, S. (1996) 'Changes in the relative demand for skills', in A. Booth and D. Snower (eds) *Acquiring skills: Market failures, their symptoms and policy responses*, Cambridge: Cambridge University Press, pp 127-46.

McKay, S. and Middleton, S. (1998) *Characteristics of older workers*, DSS Research Report No RR45, London: The Stationery Office.

Meghir, C. and Whitehouse, E. (1995) *Labour market transitions and retirement of men in the UK*, Institute for Fiscal Studies Working Paper No W95/10, London: IFS.

O'Reilly, J. (1994) 'Part-time work and employment regulation: Britain and France in the context of Europe', in M. White (ed) *Unemployment and public policy in a changing labour market*, London: Policy Studies Institute.

OECD (Organisation for Economic Co-operation and Development) (1995) *The transition from work to retirement*, Social Policy Studies No 16, Paris: OECD.

Parker, S. (1980) *Older workers and retirement*, London: HMSO.

PIU (Performance and Innovation Unit) (2000) *Winning the generation game*, London: PIU, Cabinet Office.

Reskin, B. and Roos, P. (1990) *Job queues, gender queues: Explaining women's inroads into male occupations*, Philadelphia, PA: Temple University Press.

Rubery, J. (1998) *Women in the labour market: A gender equality perspective*, V6, No 75, Paris: OECD.

Smeaton, D. (1992) *Self employment – Some preliminary findings*, Centre for Economic Performance Discussion Paper No 96, London: London School of Economics and Political Science.

Tanner, S. (1997) 'The dynamics of retirement behaviour', in R. Disney, E. Grundy and P. Johnson (eds) *The dynamics of retirement: Analyses of the retirement surveys*, DSS Research Report No 72, London: The Stationery Office, pp 25-72.

Tanner, S. (1998) 'The dynamics of male retirement behaviour', *Fiscal Studies*, vol 19, no 2, pp 175-96.

Taylor, P. and Urwin, P. (1999) 'Recent trends in the labour force participation of older people in the UK', *The Geneva Papers on Risk and Insurance*, vol 24, no 4, pp 551-79.

Taylor, P. and Urwin, P. (2001) 'Age and participation in vocational education and training', *Work, Employment & Society*, vol 15, no 4, pp 763-79

Taylor, P. and Walker, A. (1994) 'The ageing workforce: employers' attitudes towards older workers', *Work, Employment & Society*, vol 8, no 4, pp 569-91.

Taylor, P. and Walker, A. (1995) 'Utilising older workers', *Employment Gazette*, April, pp 141-5.

Taylor, P., Tillsley, C., Beausoleil, J., Wilson, R. and Walker, A. (2000) *Factors affecting retirement behaviour: A literature review*, DfEE Research Brief No 236, London: DfEE.

Tilly, C. (1996) *Half a job: Bad and good part time jobs in a changing labour market*, Philadelphia, PA: Temple University Press.

Walker, A. (1985) 'Early retirement: release or refuge from the labour market?', *Quarterly Journal of Social Affairs*, vol 1, pp 211-29.

Walker, A. and Taylor, P. (1993) 'Ageism versus productive ageing: the challenge of age discrimination in the labour market', in S. Bass, F. Caro and Y.-P. Chen (eds) *Achieving a productive ageing society*, London: Auburn House.

White, M. and Forth, J. (1998) *Pathways through unemployment: The effects of a flexible labour market*, York: Joseph Rowntree Foundation.

Appendix: Regression models of training and earnings

Table A.1: Logistic regression on training received in past three months

Variable	Full sample	Men 50+	Women 50+
Part-time	−0.159***	−0.075	−0.355**
Contract (ref=permanent)			
Temporary: fixed-term	−0.020	−0.304	0.158
Temporary: casual	0.001	−0.220	−0.680**
Temporary: agency	−0.401***	−0.132	−1.273**
Health problem	−0.154***	−0.246	0.261
Age	−0.054***	−0.065***	−0.046*
A² (age squared)	0.0004***		
Highest qualification (ref=no qualifications)			
NVQ 1 (GCSE D-G)	0.192***	0.717**	0.068
NVQ 2 (GCSE A-C)	0.401***	0.853***	0.582***
NVQ 3 (A level)	0.322***	0.867***	0.539**
NVQ 4 (higher)	0.465***	0.981***	0.165
NVQ 5 (degree)	0.461***	0.993***	0.743**
Occupation (ref=managers and administrators)			
Professionals	0.618***	0.099	0.394
Associate professionals	0.543	−0.013	0.887***
Clerical and secretarial	−0.020	−0.015	−0.019
Craft and related	−0.199**	−0.473	−0.988
Personal and protective	0.050	−0.117	−0.104
Sales	−0.043	0.189	−0.032
Plant and machine operatives	−0.724***	−0.529	−0.573
Other	−0.594***	−0.093	−0.992***
Public sector	0.549***	0.745***	0.839***
Marital status (married/cohabiting)	−0.096**	0.225	−0.268
Gender (women)	0.006		
Constant	0.225	1.02	1.22
N	18,740	1,569	1,464

Sample: Respondents changing jobs in previous year.

Notes: *p<.10, **p<.05, ***p<.01.

Source: LFS panel data

Table A.2: Determinants of hourly earnings: employees and self-employed

Variable	Effect on gross hourly pay (£)
Status (ref=self-employed professional or limited business owner)	
Self-employed: own account	−6.927***
Self-employed: subcontractor	−6.061***
Self-employed: freelancer	−1.803
Employee	−4.857***
Occupation (ref=managers and professionals)	
Clerical, secretarial and sales	−3.45***
Craft and related	−2.83***
Personal and protective	−4.03***
Plant operatives and other unskilled	−3.59***
Women	−1.74***
Age	0.466***
A^2 (age squared)	−0.005***
Employment break in previous 5 years	−0.440*
Tenure (years in job)	0.072***
Full-time	0.323
Use computer at work	1.36***
Highest qualification (ref=no qualifications)	
CSE/O level	0.267
A/AS level	1.42***
Degree or equivalent	2.89***
Constant	6.65
N	1,928

Notes: *p<.10, **p<.05, ***p<.01.

Source: WiB 2000

Table A.3: OLS regression on gross hourly pay

Variable	Full sample	Men 50+	Women 50+
Part-time	−0.757***	−0.317	−0.832***
Contract (ref=permanent)			
Temporary: fixed term	0.123	1.29**	0.773**
Temporary: casual	−0.264**	−0.821	0.706
Temporary: agency	−1.384***	−0.368	0.002
Years with company	0.101***	0.097***	0.073***
Health problem	−0.775***	−1.19***	−0.504***
Age	0.386***	−0.138***	−0.047***
A^2 (age squared)	−0.004***		
Highest qualification (ref=no qualifications)			
NVQ 1 (GCSE D-G)	0.868***	0.727***	0.590***
NVQ 2 (GCSE A-C)	1.73***	2.72***	1.37***
NVQ 3 (A level)	2.18***	1.92***	1.61***
NVQ 4 (degree)	4.02***	4.84***	4.51***
NVQ 5 (higher degree)	6.87***	8.90***	6.33***
Public sector	0.020	−0.413**	0.531***
Marital status (married/cohabiting)	0.559***	0.628***	−0.012
Gender (women)	−1.45***		
Industry (coefficients all sig*** not reported)			
Constant	−2.19	11.11	6.66
N	69,409	8,409	7,328

Notes: *p<.10, **p<.05, ***p<.01.

Source: LFS panel data

Table A.4: Logit regression on denial of a 10-minute break without permission

Variable	Full sample	Men	Women
Part-time	0.356**	0.207	0.438**
Contract (ref=permanent)			
Temporary: fixed term	−0.399	−0.818	−0.063
Temporary: casual	1.645***	0.917	2.14***
Temporary: agency	0.312	0.390	0.085
Years with company	0.001	0.008	−0.004
Public sector	0.299**	0.625***	0.009
Age	−0.014**	−0.138***	−0.001
Class (ref=higher professional/managerial)			
Lower professional/managerial	1.30***	1.11***	1.35***
Higher non-manual	0.854***	1.35***	0.575*
Lower non-manual	2.63***	2.15***	2.56***
Manual	1.79***	2.01***	1.45***
Union absent	−0.603***	−0.434**	−0.756***
Industry (ref=manufacturing, utilities, engineering)			
Construction	−0.583	−0.356	
Services	−0.271	−0.161	−0.550**
Agricultural	−0.451	−0.896	0.344
Gender (women)	0.422***		
Constant	−2.31	−2.09	−1.04
N	1,952	955	988

Notes: *p<.10, **p<.05, ***p<.01.

Source: WiB 2000

Also available in the Transitions after 50 series
Published in association with the Joseph Rowntree Foundation

The pivot generation
Informal care and work after fifty
Ann Mooney and June Statham
This topical report explores how decisions about work are affected by caring responsibilities for people aged over 50. It draws together information from a variety of sources – an analysis of trends in employment at the household level over the past twenty years, a survey of employees and those who have recently retired in both a rural and an urban area, and over 30 in-depth interviews with people over 50 – to examine the extent of caring responsibilities and how they affect choices about the timing of retirement or reducing hours of work.

Paperback £11.95 tbc ISBN 1 86134 402 3

Early retirement and income in later life
Pamela Meadows
There is growing concern about the tendency for retirement from paid employment to take place before state pension age. One of the uncertainties is whether people who retire early have sufficient financial resources to support themselves through possibly thirty or more years of retirement. This report compares the financial position of people in the current pensioner population who retired early with their counterparts who retired at state pension age. *Early retirement and income in later life* will be of interest to all those studying, researching or working in the area of pensions and retirement.

Paperback £10.95 ISBN 1 86134 442 2

Income in later life
Work history matters
Elena Bardasi and Stephen Jenkins
Until now, little has been known about the relationships between older people's incomes and their work history patterns, and how these are mediated by other factors such as gender, partnerships, ill-health and disability. This report draws on data from the British Household Panel Survey to fill these gaps. The report is one of the few UK studies about incomes in later life that uses longitudinal data as well as information about work histories. It will be of interest to researchers and policy analysts who study incomes in later life, retirement and work careers.

Paperback £12.95 ISBN 1 86134 401 5

For further information about these and other titles published by The Policy Press,
please visit our website at: www.policypress.org.uk or telephone +44 (0)117 331 4054

To order, please contact:
Marston Book Services
PO Box 269
Abingdon
Oxon OX14 4YN
UK Tel: +44 (0)1235 465500
Fax: +44 (0)1235 465556
E-mail: direct.orders@marston.co.uk

Outlawing age discrimination
Foreign lessons, UK choices
Zmira Hornstein, Sol Encel, Morley Gunderson and David Neumark
The UK is committed to legislating against age discrimination in employment and, under the EC Directive on Equal Treatment in Employment and Occupation, is expected to have legislation in place by December 2003. This important study looks at what can usefully be learned from other countries' experiences and analyses the options for the UK. It identifies legislation against age discrimination in employment in 13 countries, and looks in detail at Australia, Canada and the United States where legislation has been established for some time.

Paperback £14.95 ISBN 1 86134 354 X

Forging a new future
The expereinces and expectations of people leaving paid work over 50
Helen Barnes, Jane Parry amd Jane Lakey
Over one third of people over the age of 50 and under 65 are no longer in paid work. For some, this is a positive choice that allows them freedom to choose how to spend their time. For others, who may not have chosen to leave work, their options may be limited by income, health, caring responsibilities, or where they live.

Paperback £11.95 ISBN 1 86134 447 3

Transitions from work to retirement
Developing a new social contract
Chris Phillipson
People over the age of 50 now make up a significant proportion of the UK population. Transitions in this age group are increasingly complex, with work-based identities running alongside, or being interchanged with, leisure, caring, volunteering, and related activities. This report provides a detailed overview of the various transitions affecting people in their fifties and beyond.

Paperback £11.95 ISBN 1 86134 457 0

New policies for older people
Chris Phillipson

Against a background of population ageing, policy makers in the majority of industrialised countries are developing policies aimed at extending working life and promoting the benefits of employing older workers. This report reviews developments in several countries and offers recommendations for public policy. Based on a review of recent literature and interviews with experts in Australia, Finland, Germany, Japan, the Netherlands and the USA, this report will be invaluable reading for policy makers, practitioners and campaigners.

Paperback £13.95 ISBN 1 86134 463 5